THEATRICAL TRAINING
DURING THE AGE OF SHAKESPEARE

THEATRICAL TRAINING
DURING THE AGE OF SHAKESPEARE

David Edgecombe

Studies in Theatre Arts
Volume 2

The Edwin Mellen Press
Lewiston/Queenston/Lampeter

Library of Congress Cataloging-in-Publication Data

Edgecombe, David.
    Theatrical training during the age of Shakespeare / David
Edgecombe.
        p.   cm. -- (Studies in theatre arts ; v. 2)
    Includes bibliographical references and index.
    ISBN 0-7734-8881-2
    1. Shakespeare, William, 1564-1616--Stage history--To 1625.
2. Shakespeare, William, 1564-1616--Knowledge--Performing arts.
3. Acting--Study and teaching--England--History--16th century.
4. Shakespeare, William, 1564-1616--Study and teaching. 5. Children
as actors--England--History--16th century. 6. Theater--England-
-History--16th century. I. Title. II. Series.
PR3095.E34 1995
822.3'3--dc20   95-17480
                                              CIP

> This is volume 2 in the continuing series
> Studies in Theatre Arts
> Volume 2 ISBN 0-7734-8881-2
> STA Series ISBN 0-88946-9721-8

A CIP catalog record for this book is available from the British Library.

Copyright © 1995 David Edgecombe

All rights reserved. For information contact

The Edwin Mellen Press   The Edwin Mellen Press
Box 450   Box 67
Lewiston, New York   Queenston, Ontario
USA 14092-0450   CANADA L0S 1L0

The Edwin Mellen Press, Ltd.
Lampeter, Dyfed, Wales
UNITED KINGDOM SA48 7DY

Printed in the United States of America

DEDICATION

To my parents, Percy W. Edgecombe and Rosamund Edgecombe
and to my wife, Elizabeth Ware

TABLE OF CONTENTS

ACKNOWLEDGEMENTS

My sincere thanks go to my colleagues in theatres and educational institutions who have helped and encouraged me during the writing of this book. I especially want to thank the faculty and staff of the Department of Theatre and Dance at the University of Alaska Anchorage. This book would not have been possible without a Faculty Development Grant from that institution. A special recognition goes to the staff, board and audiences of the Indiana Shakespeare Festival for giving me the opportunity to direct Shakespeare's plays for more than a decade.

Chapters of this book have been previously published in the *Northwest Drama Review* and *The Indiana Theatre Bulletin*. Sections of other chapters were delivered as papers at national and regional meetings of the American Theatre Association and the Association for Theatre in Higher Education. The research librarians at the Folger Shakespeare Library helped immeasurably by allowing me access to many rare manuscripts. Finally, I want to thank my students who read and criticized drafts of these chapters.

CHAPTER I

THE EDUCATION OF WILLIAM SHAKESPEARE:
INDICATIONS OF FUTURE ACHIEVEMENT
IN THE DRAMATIC ARTS

Shakespeare's biographers have long complained about the paucity of information that has come down to us about the playwright's personal history. To be sure, Shakespeare never wrote an autobiography, and no contemporary account of his life has survived -- if indeed such an account ever existed. On the other hand we know more about him than most Elizabethan playwrights. Of Thomas Dekker, for example, who wrote more than forty popular plays, we know absolutely nothing except that a Thomas Dekker (who may or may not have been the same man) was buried at St. James' Clerken on August 25, 1632.

With Shakespeare's personal history, however, we are on a firm ground. Through available records we can roughly outline the important details of Shakespeare's early years. We know that such a man existed in a township of Stratford, and we are able to estimate his birth and death dates. There seems to be nothing extraordinary about his middle class background or his public school education. This has made many scholars reluctant to accept this "commoner" as the author of the immortal works. A nobel birth with its private tutelage would have justified his genius in their eyes. The evidence indicates, however, that Shakespeare was a typical English boy of the late sixteenth century, and his genius was fostered by an exceptional public educational system. We must view his achievements in terms of that social context.

Any youth's education starts well before he enters school. Shakespeare's mother, Mary, must have played a dominant role in his early development. She came from a prominent Catholic family. The Ardens could boast one of the most honored and ancient names in Warwickshire. Mary could trace her lineage back to the time of the Norman conquests. Many branches of her family were extremely wealthy and retained their nobel titles.[1] No painting of Mary was included in the inventory of the Shakespeare estate at the death of her husband, so we have no visual record of this important figure.[2] There is evidence that she was an intelligent, responsible woman: she was named the executor of her father's will although she was the youngest of his children.[3] She was probably educated and able to read and write although nothing written in her hand has survived. She is said to have married slightly below her class, which may have served to equalize her in her husband's eyes, but again, we know very little about their relationship.

John Shakespeare was almost a decade older than his wife and was known throughout the Stratford community as a hard working merchant. His name only appears once in the court records of the small town. He was accused and fined for making a "muckhill" on public property near his home -- in short he dumped some garbage.[4] Fines of this type were very common in Elizabethan England, and many communities depended on the income from these minor offenses to finance the local bureaucracy. What is surprising about this is that John was only cited once during his life. Many gentlemen of Stratford are mentioned repeatedly. Those who chose not to attend church also paid small allotments to the town council, but William's father was never charged.[5] Further proof of his position in the community is the record of his steady rise in local politics. He was first appointed "ale taster" as a young man. This was a rather prestigious position in

---

[1] S. Scheonbaum, *William Shakespeare: A Compact Documentary Life*, (New York: Oxford University Press, 1977), p. 19.

[2] Ivor Brown, *The Women in Shakespeare's Life*, (New York: Coward McCann, Inc., 1969), p. 13.

[3] Marchette Chute, *Shakespeare of London*, (New York: E.P. Dutton and Company, 1949), p. 7.

[4] Brown, *The Women in Shakespeare's Life*, p. 24.

[5] Chute, *Shakespeare of London*, p. 10.

those years and can be compared to a modern health official; he insured that the quality of the product of the local brewers was fit for human consumption. This post helped acquaint him with the people in power. With their help he quickly climbed the political ladder in Stratford. He was elected constable in 1558, Town Chamberlain in 1561 and Bailiff in 1568. This last office was the equivalent of mayor and gave John ultimate authority in the local government.[6] In spite of this public service, the elder Shakespeare never completed his application to receive the title of "gentlemen." For some reason he neglected to pursue this honor although we have every indication that it was his for the asking.

John Shakespeare was an intelligent man who must have possessed a keen air of authority. There can be little doubt that he was the dominant personality and was also dominant in his home. By trade he was a glovemaker, and since gloves were a popular accessory to stylish dress, the Shakespeare family could be considered affluent. His daily chores not only involved the selling of his products, but also the slaughtering of animals and tanning of their hides.[7] Some scholars have maintained that he was illiterate. It has often been noted that he signed his name with a picture of his trade, two crossed compasses, but this was a very common practice among middle class merchants. The recognition of this symbol made it easy to locate the signer in the town and could be considered a kind of advertisement for his trade.[8] He was probably minimally educated. He was the son of a tenant farmer, but this meant that he was taught by the same tutor who instructed the children of the lord who owned the land. It is hard to imagine an illiterate coming to such a position of authority as Bailiff.

A mysterious change occurred in John Shakespeare's life around 1576 which has puzzled scholars ever since. For some unknown reason he stopped attending the town council meetings and avoided all religious services held in the

---

[6]Robert Speaight, *Shakespeare: The Man and His Achievement*, (New York: Stein and Day Publishers, 1977), p. 7.

[7]Schoenbaum, *William Shakespeare*, p. 31.

[8]Chute, *Shakespeare of London*, p. 6.

local church.[9] Renaissance England experienced a great deal of religious strife in the years after Henry VIII's rejection of the church of Rome. During the time of John Shakespeare this conflict between Catholic and Protestant intensified. The celebration of Mass was strictly forbidden, and all religious writing was subject to strict censorship by government officials. All liturgical works had to conform to The Book of Common Prayer. Elizabeth I was excommunicated in 1570 and this papal decree served to limit the activities of the Catholics even further.[10]

In 1583 Margaret Arden, cousin to Mary, and her husband John Somerville were arrested and executed for plotting an assignation of the Queen. They were denounced as papists and many members of their family were also affected. It is possible that repercussions of the plot were felt in Stratford, but there is no evidence of persecution directed toward any of the Shakespeares.[11] In any case, it was a time of great religious controversy. Many English citizens still adhered to the traditional rituals of the Catholic Church.

Frederick J. Pohl suggests that John Shakespeare was one of these religious traditionalists and that the reason for his separation from the community was the intensity of his belief.[12] Prior to the strict anti-papist policies of Elizabeth I, John worshipped regularly in the Catholic manner. His first child, Joan, was christened a Roman Catholic.[13] This was during the reign of Mary who had briefly tried to re-establish the outlawed liturgy in England. She met with little success. To prove the depth of John's convictions, Pohl cites a document which was found hidden above the ceiling panels in the Shakespeare family home. These pages were found in 1757, more that a century after Shakespeare's death, by a laborer who was repairing some roof tiles. Unfortunately the papers have not survived to the present, but before they were

---

[9]Schoenbaum, *William Shakespeare*, p. 39.

[10]Speaight, *Shakespeare*, pp. 8-9.

[11]Ibid., p. 23.

[12]Frederick J. Pohl, *Like to the Lark: The Early Years of Shakespeare*, (New York: Clarkson N. Potter, Inc., 1972), p. 17.

[13]Schoenbaum, *William Shakespeare*, p. 23.

lost they were authenticated by an 18th century scholar. If they are real they shed some valuable insights into the character of William's father and the playwright's struggle with religious and philosophical issues which are central themes to some of his sonnets. The pages contained a transcription in long hand of a Catholic prayer which was given to those whose faith was being shaken by outside forces. It was meant to be recited to exorcise the threatening forces until the true spirituality returned. Pohl gives a picture of John as a man obsessed by religious dogma who is unable to decide between these two sects of Christianity. If the Shakespeares were living in a self-imposed exile in their own community, there must have been a marked effect on the emotional development of young William. As the son of a papist he would have been subjected to much of the slander which touched his father. If the conjecture is true, William may have grown up an outcast among his peers.[14]

William, the third child born to John and Mary, was christened an Anglican.[15] His two sisters died in early childhood. When this new boy arrived in the Shakespeare home he must have been welcomed with great joy. The date of his baptism was recorded as April 26, 1564. Since it was customary to wait three days to see if the baby lived, most scholars maintain that he was born a few days before that date. He survived a plague that ravaged Stratford that same year and grew to be a healthy child. There is no evidence to suggest that Shakespeare experienced any sickness during the early years of his life.[16]

---

[14]Schoenbaum refutes this evidence. He maintains that there is nothing to substantiate the claim that John Shakespeare was a papist. He accuses those proponents of this theory of loaded research. The testimony of Malone, the eighteenth century scholar, was made without ever seeing an example of John Shakespeare's hand writing. He believes it to be a forgery. The fact that William's father withdrew from the council and the church remains. Schoenbaum states that the reasons for his seclusion were not financial, but he offers no suggestion as to the actual motivation. Schoenbaum, *William Shakespeare*, p. 42.

[15]Speaight, *Shakespeare*, p. 7.

[16]Ivor Brown, *How Shakespeare Spent the Day*, (New York: Hill and Wang, 1963), p. 187.

Stratford laws were rather strict for those under the age of fifteen. Children had to be off the streets by eight o'clock in the evening.[17] Because of the extended school hours, their playtime was very limited. Young William most likely spent much of his free time working in his father's shop. Even holidays were business days for the local merchants. During festivals stalls were set up in the town square. While his father sold his leather goods, William had a chance to observe the celebrations. This must have been his first exposure to the performing arts. Many traveling troupes of actors and performers were commissioned by the local governments to supply the entertainment during these feast days. Because the law required all actors to be "gainfully employed" most companies were "sponsored" -- that is, they were considered servants of the nobility. Although itinerant minstrels were common throughout the English countryside, they were considered outlaws and could be punished with imprisonment. All those players who appeared in Stratford had to be licensed by the Bailiff, and there are many records of John Shakespeare granting permission to these traveling theatrical companies.[18] Although Stratford was not near any of the major highways of Elizabethan England, it became a popular place for these performances. It is quite possible that John's patronage helped promote the appreciation of the arts in his community, and William's exposure to dramatics must have been considerable.

Young William probably engaged in many of the traditional games of the period. Many of these childhood pastimes are mentioned in his plays. Some of the most typical are still being played in altered versions by modern children. "Hoodman-blind" was very similar to our "blind-man's-bluff" except for the increased violence. Many times the "hoodman" was prodded with sticks until he was lucky enough to strike one of his comrades.[19] Other physical games

---

[17]Chute, *Shakespeare of London*, p. 2.

[18]Pohl, *Like to the Lark*, p. 14.

[19]Alan Dent, *World of Shakespeare: Sports and Pastimes*, (New York: Taplinger Publishing Company, 1974), p. 28.

included "Running the Gauntlet", balancing on a barrel, stave fighting and wrestling.[20] These Elizabethan games were treated very seriously by the participants and encouraged by the parents. Physical conditioning and a knowledge of hand-to-hand combat were important to the English man of honor. These skills were introduced in childhood and refined in later life. There is evidence to indicate that the young Shakespeare also trained in the more cultural pursuits. He was probably never taught to play a musical instrument, although as seen in his plays, he later acquired a passing knowledge of music theory.[21]

William's formal education began when he was four or five years old.[22] He attended the public school which offered a tuition-free education without class distinction. His father's social and financial position would narrow the possibilities of education for William, but the school in Stratford was one of the finest of its type in England. The building itself was built by the Guild of the Holy Cross and completed in the early fifteenth century. This organization was a philanthropic guild of Catholic men supported by endowments from the community. For several centuries they enjoyed considerable power in England. Many buildings in Stratford, including the town council meeting hall were built by the Guild.[23] The accumulated wealth of this organization was confiscated by the crown under the Chantries Act of Edward VI. The Guild of the Holy Cross was disbanded and all its property became the possession of the crown. In 1553 the Common Council of Stratford regained some of the funds and the title to the schoolhouse. It was renamed the King's New School but continued the same educational standards.[24]

---

[20]Pohl, *Like to the Lark*, p. 15.

[21]Brown, *How Shakespeare Spent the Day*, p. 119.

[22]Schoenbaum, *William Shakespeare*, p. 63.

[23]Ibid., p. 7.

[24]Virgil K. Whitaker, *Shakespeare's Use of Learning*, (San Marino, California: The Huntington Library Press, 1953), p. 14.

8

The school hours were long and gave the student little time for himself. Classes began at 5:45 a.m. in the summer and 6:45 a.m. in the winter.[25] There was an 11:00 "breakfast" recess and classes began again about 1:00. Study continued until 6:00 in the evening, leaving the children only two hours before the curfew call. Thursdays and Saturdays were half holidays.[26] This intensive schedule of study instilled a sense of discipline in the Elizabethan child. William's early education was supervised not by the principle schoolmaster, but by an usher who worked for him. He spared the Master "that tedious trouble", as the council described it, of "teaching the young youth."[27] The usher was usually a young man of the community who was paid to teach Latin grammar to those under the age of seven. Often the ushers were not very well educated. It proved exceedingly difficult for some schools to find ushers, not surprising considering their pay scale. An usher made about four pounds a year -- a small amount even for those times.[28] The master was paid about twenty pounds a year and usually a place to live. This was a comfortable wage and was far higher than teachers in the larger cities would receive for a similar position. In Stratford the master had to pay the salary of the usher, but this expenditure still left him with a good wage for himself.[29]

Because of the high pay and benefits, the position of schoolmaster attracted some highly qualified teachers. Simon Hunt was schoolmaster when William started the "upper school", or when he moved over from the usher's class to be taught by the master. Simon Hunt took over from Walter Roche and was in turn replaced by Thomas Jenkins when Hunt left teaching to become a Jesuit priest. All three were Oxford graduates. The equivalent today would be a Yale Ph.D. teaching on a secondary level. These teachers were far superior to

---

[25]Speaight, *Shakespeare*, p. 11.

[26]Schoenbaum, *William Shakespeare*, p. 67.

[27]Ibid., p. 63.

[28]Whitaker, *Shakespeare's Use of Learning*, pp. 14-15.

[29]Chute, *Shakespeare of London*, p. 19.

their counterparts in the big cities.[30] When better offers came they were usually accepted. Thomas Jenkins left when William was about fifteen. He was recorded as having sold his position for six pounds to John Cotton, "late of London."[31] This happened in 1579 and Shakespeare continued to attend grammar school for another year. The three years he spent under the tutelage of Thomas Jenkins were concentrated with study, and it is safe to assume that this teacher was a great influence on young William Shakespeare.

Educational techniques of Elizabethan England were conservative -- a holdover from the cloistered study of the Middle Ages. One writer described William's education as "thorough, serious and dull."[32] No one tried to educate a student for ordinary life, that was handled in his apprenticeship if it was approached at all. The student from a very early age was taught to read, write and recite Latin. About a decade after Shakespeare attended school some scholars were encouraging that English also be added to the curriculum. These recommendations were ignored.[33]

> In the first place, the pupil was expected to learn by intensive drill upon a very small body of material, generally memorizing it verbatim... The child was not expected to master much, but what he did was study on an adult level of ideas.[34]

Almost all their lessons had to be memorized, and this included many parts of the Book of Common Prayer and the Bible. Religion and education were inseparable. Catechism, the Lord's Prayer and the Apostles' Creed were all part of the Latin daily recitation. Although the method was tedious, it did perfect the students' vocal skills at a relatively young age.

Textbooks and writing materials were scarce and expensive. This fact meant that the younger students might only see a few books during their "lower

---

[30]Whitaker, *Shakespeare's Use of Learning*, p. 15.
[31]Ibid.
[32]Chute, *Shakespeare of London*, p. 15.
[33]Ibid.
[34]Whitaker, *Shakespeare's Use of Learning*, p. 15.

school" education. Their first book was not really a book at all, it was a "hornbook." Though we generally associate this with a later age, hornbooks were the introductory text for young students from the Middle Ages until the beginning of the eighteenth century. The hornbook was a wooden tablet with a carved handle. The printed surface was covered with a thin piece of animal horn to protect the writing from the smudges of little hands. These books were almost indestructible and could be used over and over again. Across the top of this printed page were rows of letters in different type faces. Then came a list of vowels and the elements of syllabification. Finally an example of writing was included. This was usually an invocation to the Trinity and the Lord's Prayer.[35] Many of the rules of Latin grammar had to be communicated orally. This meant that William became verbally proficient long before he was able to read the language.

The students studied one other book with the usher. During the time of Shakespeare this volume was called "The ABCs with Catechism." This became a standardized title although the authors and the content changed. This soft bound book contained about twenty to thirty pages of sample alphabets, examples of scripture and other writings. The students were able to apply the lessons of the hornbook to the readings supplied by the "ABCs." Although the resources were meager, to say the least, most students acquired a workable knowledge of Latin by the time they were ten years old.[36] Other writers read exclusively in Latin included Aesop, Terence and some Plautus. The last playwright seems of particular interest to our young student. Shakespeare's early work draws heavily from these classics. Most of this exposure was supplied by the Master in the upper-school.[37]

---

[35]Schoenbaum, *William Shakespeare*, p. 63.

[36]Chute, *Shakespeare of London*, p. 14.

[37]Whitaker, *Shakespeare's Use of Learning*, p. 22.

Around 1574 or 1575 William Shakespeare graduated from the lower school to the upper school. It is safe to assume that he had Thomas Jenkins as his teacher.[38] Jenkins followed the trends in education and introduced his students to a select number of Latin poets. The favorites were Ovid and Quintilian.[39] Of these, Shakespeare's favorite was Ovid, judging from the allusions in his scripts. Later he seemed to prefer to read the classics in English translation: he drew on them constantly. Many of his plays are based on the mythology of Ovid's *Metamorphoses*.[40] He also studied rhetoric in Cicero's *Rhetorica ad C. Herennium*. This text introduced him to many of the terms of English law.[41] Other sources which Shakespeare drew on heavily for his plays included: Lily's *Latin Grammar*, Holinshed's *Chronicles of England*, and of course the *Geneva Bible*. Lily's text is a simple introduction to some of the grammatical rules of the language. He probably first saw this book in the upper school in Stratford, but, as evidence in his play scripts, it served him as a source throughout his writing career. Holinshed's *Chronicles* may have been Shakespeare's exclusive source for all the plots of his English history plays. Although he may have consulted other sources, the basic outline was invariably drawn from Holinshed. He was introduced to this volume in the upper school and one can imagine that he carried it in his pack when he finally journeyed to London.[42] *The Geneva Bible* was the accepted translation of the scriptures recognized by the Church of England. It was also called the "Breeches Bible" because the Book of Genesis contains this translation of a famous passage: "... and they sewed fig leaves together and made themselves breeches."[43]

---

[38]Schoenbaum, *William Shakespeare*, p. 70.

[39]Whitaker, *Shakespeare's Use of Learning*, p. 28.

[40]Chute, *Shakespeare of London*, p. 16.

[41]Whitaker, *Shakespeare's Use of Learning*, p. 28.

[42]Speaight, *Shakespeare*, p. 12.

[43]George A. Plimpton, *The Education of Shakespeare*, (London: Oxford University Press, 1933), p. 57.

It is ironic that the one skill which gave the Bard his immortality was the least emphasized in his public school education. The art of writing Latin was postponed until late in the upper school curriculum. Part of the slowness of teaching writing may have been caused by the cost of paper. Paper was not manufactured at all in England until the sixteenth century, and the cost of imported paper was heavy.[44] Many schools required their students to supply their own writing supplies. The cost of these accessories made many students unable to participate in this part of their studies. From what we know of John Shakespeare, it is obvious that William had pen and paper when they were required.

The course in writing began with instruction on how to make a pen. The tedious task of selecting a quill, cutting the point and curing the end is a chore which modern mass production has spared our students, but for the Elizabethans this was vital knowledge. From the examples of Shakespeare's signature which have survived, it seems that William was not a dedicated student of penmanship. This lack of legibility concerned him very little, but it must have complicated the task of the compilers of the First Folio.[45]

The advanced students received instruction on both formal and informal writing. Letter writing was covered by the master and included a brief lesson on the compilation of love letters. Poetry in these matters was taught to be "second only to decorum", and Shakespeare "learned his lesson well."[46]

Vocal training might also be a part of the education of a young boy. Although it was not universally accepted, many scholars recommended that the voice be trained to sing a "tunable uttering."[47] This training and the concentration on rhetoric and verbal skills would seem to make dramatic performance an eventual consequence. Such was not the case however. The

---

[44]Ibid., p. 67.
[45]Ibid., p. 68.
[46]Ibid., p. 137.
[47]Chute, *Shakespeare of London*, p. 17.

reading of plays in class was rare. There is some evidence that schoolmasters allowed their students to perform the works of Plautus and Terence, but these teachers were the exception. Plays were sometimes read in the upper school, but full-scale productions were rare. There is little to indicate that Shakespeare ever participated in acting or in play production during his early years; but the exposure to those works was an important influence in the development of his skills as a writer.[48]

Lily's *Latin Grammar* concluded with a long section specifically intended for the moral instruction of the students. It is rather sententious and longwinded and may have inspired Shakespeare when he wrote Polonius' advice to Laertes. The sins of the flesh were a threat to the immortal soul of every Christian child, and it was the master's duty to impart the precepts of the Church of England.[49]

> From the first day of school no effort was spared to make him a mortal man and a Christian according to the ideas and ideals of the Church of England, and all other objectives were definitely and firmly subordinate to that main purpose.[50]

A noted educator of the time, the Headmaster of Westminster School who later became the Dean of St. Paul's, wrote a track directed to the student himself.

> For as much as the master ought to be his scholars a second parent and father, not of their bodies but of their minds, I see it belongeth to the order of my duty, my dear child, not so much to instruct thee civilly in learning and good manners, as to furnish thy mind, and that in thy tender years, with good opinions and true religion. For this age of childhood ought no less, yea also much more, to be trained with good lessons of godliness, than with good acts to humanity.[51]

Often the only English reading attempted in the classroom was from the Geneva Bible. It was up to the master to make the concepts of the Bible clear to the young. In 1547 the following recommendations were made by the commissioners of Winchester College:

---

[48]Ibid.

[49]Whitaker, *Shakespeare's Use of Learning*, p. 20.

[50]Ibid., p. 17.

[51]Schoenbaum, *William Shakespeare*, p. 62.

> From henceforth the Bible shall be daily read in English distinctly
> and appropriately, in the midst of the hall, above the hearth where the fire
> is made both at dinner and supper.[52]

Many of the secondary schools were quick to follow this lead. The Protestant

Reformation encouraged the use of translations of the holy books. Many teachers

still used the Latin texts, but by the time of Shakespeare, Bible readings were in

English.

> Every scholar shall be taught to say the Lord's Prayer, the Articles
> of Faith, the Ten Commandments, and other chief parts of the catechism
> and principle points of Christian religion, in English first and after in
> Latin, and on Sunday and holidays, the master shall read a lecture to all,
> or the most part of the scholars, which he shall think meet to hear thereof,
> out of Calvin or Nowell's work.[53]

Protestant doctrine and anti-papist propaganda were introduced carefully to the

students of the grammar schools. With the rapid reversals in religious loyalties,

many teachers were afraid to propose new theories. Even translators had to

beware of offending the religious hierarchy. In 1536 William Tyndale was

accused of "untrue translations" based on Hebrew and Greek texts. His public

execution served as a warning to those who would challenge the word of the

Roman Church. The Geneva Bible was published in 1560 and was the most

popular translation for more than fifty years. It was succeeded by the King James

Bible which was published in 1611. It is ironic that much of the groundwork for

this great translation was included in Tyndale's Bible.[54] Shakespeare's Biblical

allusions are always from the Geneva Bible.

It is possible that those who compiled the King James version had

witnessed the original productions of the Globe Theatre. As one of the most

popular playwrights of the period, Shakespeare's verse may have influenced the

poetry found in this great work. In spite of the risks of heresy, teachers undertook

---

[52]Plimpton, *The Education of Shakespeare*, p. 57.

[53]Ibid., p. 61.

[54]Introduction to *The Holy Bible* Revised Standard Version (New York: Thomas Nelson and Sons, 1952), p. iii.

the moral and spiritual education of their pupils. Many educators viewed youth as a time of great temptation. Lessons in the upper school included instruction in "releasing devil spirits." "Exorcism was to be learned because every boy was more or less full of the devil."[55]

Corporal punishment was an almost daily occurrence in the Elizabethan schoolhouse. Discipline often took the form of whippings with the entire class observing. Often the delinquent was held across a desk by four of his classmates while the teacher applied the birch.[56] Good behavior was demanded of every student no matter how young, and Christian morality was the principle educational goal.

Whatever systems were used in teaching young William, the results have been debated by a succession of critics. "No writer is more moral than Shakespeare in fundamentals."[57] We can try to discover the playwright's values by analyzing the lines his characters speak, but they may not necessarily be his. Any conclusions about William's personal religious beliefs, as distinct from religious background, is hazardous in the extreme."[58] More than likely, Shakespeare was not a pious person. He often takes a satiric look at Puritanism and religious contradictions.[59] But the implied morality behind the plots seems traditionally Christian. Both *Hamlet* and *Macbeth* struggle with the tenets of faith. In a way, Shakespeare seemed to make religious perceptions his own. The moral lessons of his childhood would dominate his thinking throughout his life.

Sundays were a day of mandatory church attendance. Sermons were often long and involved -- some lasted well into the afternoon. Before John's withdrawal, the Shakespeares were regular in their devotion. Young William must have sat transfixed by these speeches of fire and brimstone. These religious

---

[55]Speaight, *Shakespeare*, p. 12.

[56]Plimpton, *The Education of Shakespeare*, p. 47.

[57]Whitaker, *Shakespeare's Use of Learning*, p. 41.

[58]Speaight, *Shakespeare*, p. 9.

[59]*Measure for Measure* is an excellent example of this type of satire.

harangues were often fraught with drama to keep the interest of a tiring congregation.[60] There is no evidence that William continued to go to church after his father stopped, but by that time the Bard was nearing manhood. He completed his studies at the King's New School in 1580.[61] Very few Stratford residents continued their education past the upper school. Indeed the education supplied by the township of Stratford would prove more than adequate for the needs of these children. Most of them would remain in the town and assume their places in the local trade guilds. The sons of merchants would inevitably continue on as members of their father's trade. Their knowledge was notably lacking in several disciplines which would have served them well. Mathematics was almost never taught at the grammar school level. Ledgers of the period show that even officials of the town were sadly ignorant of addition, subtraction and multiplication.[62] Social science and natural science were never even approached. The students received a brief account of Rome from Plutarch and rare schools studied English History from Holinshed's *Chronicles*. The only other language read in the classroom was Greek, and this was taught as second to Latin.[63] As monodimensional as this education seems to us, it did teach dedication and discipline. The long hours of study concentrated upon a limited body of material could not help but develop patience in the Elizabethan student. For William Shakespeare his early schooling gave him a thirst for general knowledge resulting in a wealth of historical and literary detail to be found throughout his work.

The years after he left school are somewhat of a mystery to scholars. It is reasonably certain that he did not continue his studies at one of the large English universities. His family's limited income and his lack of social connections made that a virtual impossibility. These years are often referred to as the "lost years," not because they were empty, but because they have always

---

[60]Speaight, *Shakespeare*, p. 14.

[61]Plimpton, *The Education of Shakespeare*, p. 3.

[62]Chute, *Shakespeare of London*, p. 17.

[63]Whitaker, *Shakespeare's Use of Learning*, p. 37.

been filled with uncertainty. How could the son of a glover, who disappears from
our view at the age of seventeen, turn up in London at the age of twenty-four
with several completed plays? What did this man with a common education do to
acquire the theatrical expertise so necessary for the playwright's craft? The
legends assigned to this period are exciting but often misleading. The most
famous, and most commonly refuted, is the "deer poaching" episode. Even if it
were true it sheds very little light on the character of William Shakespeare.
Others would have the young man work as an apprentice at his father's trade.
Certainly the span of these years marks the traditional period of apprenticeship.

> Apprentices were not all 'boyes.' They were compelled statute to
> be twenty-four years of age before coming out of their apprenticeship, so
> that most of those in London were between seventeen and twenty-four --
> single, native-born, and mentally and physically fit.[64]

Nicholas Rowe, in his biography of Shakespeare published in 1709, states that
Shakespeare was taken from school by his father to help with the family business.

> ...and the want of his assistance at home, forced his father to
> withdraw him from thence... and to take him into his own employment...
> his father was a butcher, and I have been told heretofore by some for his
> neighbours, that when he was a boy he exercised his father's trade, but
> when he killed a calf, he would do it in high style, and make a speech.[65]

We cannot accept this a proof of his budding genius, but if he did remain at home
during these years he probably did most of the slaughtering for his father. This
kind of vocation was not the best preparation for the vocation he was to adopt in
London. Others have maintained that he may have been employed in the town of
Stratford as an usher. In this case he probably did not teach in the public school,
but may have served in one of the homes of the local nobility. It was common for
tutors to be employed for the upper class children of the time. This vocation
would have kept him in contact with the academic world and given him access to
the manor house library. Often these collections were quite extensive.[66] The

---

[64]Alfred Harbage, *Shakespeare's Audience*, (New York: Columbia University Press, 1961), p. 82.
[65]Schoenbaum, *William Shakespeare*, pp. 73-74.
[66]Schoenbaum, *William Shakespeare*, p. 95.

eighteenth century historian, Edmond Malone, suggested that Shakespeare was an apprentice to the local barrister. This highly debatable speculation he draws from an examination of the legal terms which are in abundance in the plays.[67]

One of the most plausible theories to account for the "lost years" was suggested in 1937 by Oliver Baker and is most clearly put forth by Frederick Pohl. He believes that William may have been an apprentice with a traveling theatrical troupe which performed in Lancashire. As evidence supporting this contention he sites the will of a Lancashire gentleman by the name of Alexandar Houghton. Houghton left a sizeable sum to one William Shakeshafte. Pohl maintains that this spelling is a variant of Shakespeare and cites many of William's relatives who referred to themselves in that way.[68] If the names refer to the same person, Shakespeare received a thorough, practical theatrical education before he came to London. According to Pohl, his experience would have included acting and playwriting for the troupe. It was not uncommon for such actors to produce their own scripts. Many of these pieces had to be written very quickly and tailored to the specific needs of the individual performers. Such an experience could be considered the ideal situation for an aspiring playwright. Touring not only gave him the opportunity to see his works on stage, but also to speak his own words. Shakespeare's success in playwriting would thus draw heavily from his experience as an actor. No novice could have conceived the visual humor indicated in his early plays. The confrontation between Valentine and the Duke in *The Two Gentlemen of Verona* (Act III, Scene I.) was written by a performer who understood pantomimic entertainment. This is only one example where the master manifests his talent and perception as an actor in the creation of this plays. Admittedly these early attempts at playwriting seem crude when compared to his later artistic level, but they do demonstrate that Shakespeare understood the fundamentals of popular play production.

---

[67]Ibid., p. 109.
[68]Pohl, *Like to the Lark*, p. 21.

All this must remain conjecture. Many critics doubt whether the Bard ever left Stratford during these years.[69] Certainly he would have had to return to his home town to be married to Anne Hathaway in 1582. It is hard to imagine that she would be able to foster a romance young William touring the countryside. These inconsistencies demonstrate the pitfalls of researching a preconception. Whatever the truth of the matter may be, Shakespeare obviously knew the craft of play production even before his arrival in London. Many academicians have refused to believe that this knowledge was intuitive. They spend their time searching through archives for some piece of evidence that Shakespeare was more than the common man.

Even if he never studied dramatics as a youth, his exposure to professional performances may have been extensive. From the time he was very young he witnessed some of the finest theatrical groups of Renaissance England. Whenever there was a plague in the larger cities, theatres closed their doors and entire companies went on the road, and brought entertainment and inspiration to citizens living outside the major metropolitan areas. Shakespeare saw two of the finest troupes when he was a boy: The Queen's Men and the Earl of Worchester's Men were the first to come; they played in the Guild Hall in the summer of 1560, when John Shakespeare presided as bailiff.[70]

Among the performers were some of the finest actors in England. They would return again and again before Shakespeare was to leave his home town. There is evidence that there was some type of major theatrical event in the town

---

[69]Schoenbaum feels that this theory is based on a misinterpretation of the available evidence. To him the date on the Houghton will reads "1533" and not "1588" as Pohl suggests. He also states that "Shakeshafte" is in reality "Shakeschafte." This second spelling was very common among the local populous, and Schoenbaum can find at least two examples of "William Shakeschaftes" born in the immediate area of Lancashire. He claims that from the position of this name on the document the servant had to be at least thirty-five years old at the time of this entry. Evidently beneficiaries were always listed according to their age and service. Shakespeare would have been far too young to qualify for this sizeable inheritance. Although Schoenbaum discounts all of the legends, he offers no thesis of his own to employment during the "lost years." It seems for the moment as we will have to accept that the mystery is deeper than ever. Schoenbaum, *William Shakespeare*, pp. 112-115.

[70]Ibid., p. 6.

about twice a year.[71]There is really no way to know if young William witnessed all these productions, but with his father as head magistrate he was probably present at most of them.

The plays were not strictly for adults. Often Bible stories were enacted for the moral instruction of the community. During holidays the corresponding parable was almost required by the audience. Sometimes the groups were small. When large cast classical plays were performed, often only six men would have to play twenty-five or thirty individual characters. This situation demanded much "willing suspension of disbelief" on the part of the townspeople.[72]

As a boy of fifteen he could have witnessed one of the last performances of the great cycle of Mystery Plays acted by the craft guilds in Coventry, and only a short ride from Stratford. Religion and theatre were still inter-related. It was not until the reign of Elizabeth I that liturgical drama was prohibited. If he did see such a massive production spectacle it must have made a great impression on William.[73] There is even some evidence that amateur plays were staged throughout rural England. These local productions may have been similar to the one Shakespeare later parodied in *A Midsummer Night's Dream*. Crude as they may have been, they may have educated the Bard in the devices of the stage. However there is no evidence that Shakespeare ever participated in these amateur dramatic events.[74] Knowledge of his early theatrical experience can only be based on speculation.

The inability of critics to accept Shakespeare as the author of his plays stems from the suspicion that his public school education did not match the greatness displayed in his later literary proficiency. Perhaps if he had emulated the other university-trained writers he would have met the modern critics imposed standards. Shakespeare's reputation is free from the rumors of "drinking and

---

[71]Chute, *Shakespeare of London*, p. 23.
[72]Ibid.
[73]Schoenbaum, *William Shakespeare*, p. 111.
[74]Dent, *World of Shakespeare*, p. 10.

whoring" that clouded the reputations of Marlowe and Greene.[75] This "upstart crow," in Greene's words, did not even meet the standards of his own generation. His genius was fostered in the heartland of the English countryside. He was educated in one of the finest public schools of his time, and his early plays clearly reflect the literature taught at the Stratford Grammar School. *Love's Labour's Lost* has been regarded as one of Shakespeare's earliest comedies:

> *Love's Labour's Lost* can be studied for its allusions to grammar school texts and contemporary literature even though no major source exits.[76]

When we compare the content of Elizabethan educational systems to the variety offered by educators of today, the practice of the former seems severely limited. The educational requirements taught young William the discipline necessary to compete in the world of London Theatre.

> He studied much less, but far more intensively; he was taught to memorize rather than to question or discuss. He wrote according to an approved formulae and stated the sentiments of standard authors; any originality that he might possess would find expression in the disposition of material, not in the material itself.[77]

Shakespeare's originality was not limited by these strict, standardized educational patterns. It is possible that in spite of the very dull curriculum the Elizabethan system was more effective than our modern system of education.

> Granted a very simple curriculum and a competent teacher, and granted, above all, a group of students small enough for the individual instructor to give them some personal attention, it was possible for a gifted student to progress much more rapidly under this arrangement than in the rigidly separated grades that American efficiency has imposed upon the school system.[78]

The small size of William's class and the lack of class levels allowed each student to progress at his own rate. At first glance this type of individualized

---

[75]A.L. Rowse, Introduction to *The Annotated Shakespeare*, (New York: Clark N. Potter, Inc., 1978), p. 10.

[76]Whitaker, *Shakespeare's Use of Learning*, p. 7.

[77]Ibid., p. 36.

[78]Whitaker, *Shakespeare's Use of Learning*, pp. 15-16.

education may seen to have advantages, but the effectiveness was solely dependent on one factor -- the quality of the instructor. It is safe to assume that Shakespeare's principle instructor, Thomas Jenkins, was a thorough, stimulating teacher. His student's early works demonstrate the depth of learning and testify to his expertise.

Shakespeare's art indicates that the man behind the work was more than a dry academician. The Bard's classroom was life. The depth of experience revealed in his plays shows that the years following his formal education were full indeed. He was never exclusively a bookworm, rather he was a "poet of open air."[79] His love for life and nature are clearly manifested in the pages of his plays. Since he never attended a university, the "lost years" gave him an opportunity to experience the world he had heretofore only known in books.

---

[79]Speaight, *Shakespeare*, p. 16.

CHAPTER II

THE TRAINING OF THE APPRENTICES

IN SHAKESPEARE'S COMPANY

Although many Elizabethan actors achieved fame during their lifetimes, we know relatively little about the lives of the apprentices. In most cases, we know them by name only.

> Most frustrating is our almost complete ignorance of the boys who played the great female roles that have since tested, and often defeated, the abilities of famous actresses.[80]

The young actors rarely became famous "start" performers. Often their names would not even appear on the playbills. No portrait exists of any apprentice, and we have no reason to believe that many were even painted.[81]

The reasons for keeping these young artists in obscurity are complex. The Puritans viewed theatrical performances with disdain. Actors were thought to be aligned with the devil.

> To demand reward for this idle way of living was to be guilty of a kind of dishonesty, cheating or filching money gained by the labor of others. Acting was not recognized as a commodity, entertainments should be free and spontaneous; so players were freely compared both with thieves and with whores.[82]

In spite of the church's vehement denunciations of the actor's craft, London theatre was extremely popular. Drama was particularly popular with the young apprentices from the professional guilds. They came by the hundreds for

---

[80]Clifford Leech, *The Revels History of Drama in English*, 3 volumes, (London: Methuen and Company, 1957), II:108.

[81]Ivor Brown, *Shakespeare and the Actors*, (London: The Bodley Head, 1970), p. 97.

[82]M.C. Bradbrook, *The Rise of the Common Player: A Study of Actor and Society in Shakespeare's England*, (Cambridge, Mass.: Harvard University Press, 1961), p. 47.

the afternoon performances and paid a penny to stand in the pit.[83] Although a law was passed in 1542 forbidding all apprentices and journeymen from attending any public entertainment, it seemed not to have been enforced.[84] Some years later the Puritan ministers were to attack this practice from the pulpit. On August 24, 1578, J. Stockwood preached in a sermon:

> Flocks of wild youths of both sexes, resorting to interludes, where both by lively gesture and voices there are allurements unto whoredom.[85]

The rising influence of religious conservatism, however, could not quell the interest of the youth. Nor did it discourage young actors from seeking apprenticeships with the professional performers. There was a long history of training young in the dramatic arts which extends far back into the middle ages. Itinerant minstrels and traveling troupes usually had at least one apprentice who played the women's roles and probably acted as a servant.

The apprentices were generally respected by most of London society. They were often the sons of landed gentlemen from estates throughout England, and they had been sent to the city to learn a trade. In the ranks of these apprentices were future mayors and judges.[86] They were usually well-educated; their education often continued through their apprenticeship. The arrangement between master and apprentice was more than monetary. The student would live for many years with his employer's family.

> It was an essential feature of the medieval system that the apprentice should reside with the master, whose duty it was to instill social virtues into the as well as to teach him knowledge of the craft.[87]

Only after the eighteenth century did a wage/work arrangement become the exclusive part of the apprentice contract. The Master became the boy's adopted

---

[83]Chute, *Shakespeare of London*, p. 38.

[84]Bradbrook, *The Rise of the Common Player*, p. 44.

[85]Ibid., p. 101.

[86]Chute, *Shakespeare of London*, p. 39.

[87]L.C. Knights, *Drama and Society in the Age of Jonson*, (London: Chatto and Windus, Ltd., 1937), p. 42.

parents, in a manner of speaking. In return for his work, the apprentice was given food and shelter.

The theatrical apprentices shared the same system as their peers in the other guilds. One critic, Stephen Gosson, wrote unfavorably about the training of actors (1582).

> Most of the players have been either men of occupations, which they have forsaken to live by playing, or common minstrels, or trained up from childhood to this abominable exercise, and have no other way to get their living.[88]

Most would start their apprenticeship between the ages of ten and sixteen. Their training would continue until they were well into their early twenties. Most young men had completed their contracts by the time they were twenty-four.[89] Although we have no evidence that he was an apprentice, Richard Burbage started acting at the age of thirteen. We know that some of the young actors continued to play women's roles well into their twenties.[90]

The apprentices were at the bottom of the organizational ladder at the Globe Theatre. The housekeepers were at the top. They owned the theatre building and received most of the profits from the daily performances. The thirty-two shares of theatre stock were divided between the housekeepers and the principle actors in the company. During the reign of Elizabeth I, Shakespeare, Richard Burbage, John Heminges and Henry Condel each owned four shares for a total of sixteen, or half. The remaining sixteen were distributed among the other actors. Only stockholders could share in the cash receipts from the ticket sales. Smaller parts were played by journeymen who were hired specifically for a role. Their contract usually expired when the production closed. They were paid by the

---

[88]Bernard Beckerman, *Shakespeare at the Globe: 1599-1609*, (New York: The MacMillan Company, 1962), p. 122.

[89]C. Walter Hodges, *Shakespeare and the Players*, (London: G. Bell and Sons, 1970), p. 43.

[90]Andrew Gurr, *The Shakespearean Stage: 1574-1642*, (London: The Cambridge University Press, 1970), p. 69.

housekeepers for their services.[91] The only unpaid workers at the theatre were the apprentices, although sometimes they did receive money from their master for the purchase of clothing. There is a notation in the Henslowe diary which complains about the exorbitant cost of keeping them dressed.[92]

The apprentices were not the responsibility of the company, as they were in the professional boy troupes; they were wards of individual actors.[93] They were literally considered "property" and had no rights outside of those given to them by their masters. Once they entered into an indentureship, there was little hope of escape for an unhappy apprentice. A touching account is found in the Folger Library. Supposedly, this tract was written by a young apprentice, one Peter Moore, on the eve of his execution for the crime of murdering his master, Humphrey Bidgood. In this paper Moore confesses that he poisoned the man with white lead to escape his contract of indenture. The pamphlet takes the form of a lecture to all the apprentices of London. It warns them to obey and respect their masters or else the same fate would befall them.[94]

Apprentices often resisted the controls of their masters. Riots by gangs of these young wards were common in Elizabethan England, and on at least one occasion the participants received capital punishment for their offenses. An excellent account of such a riot is found in the Folger Library. It was published by William Blackwall in 1595 and ends with a stern admonition of apprentices in general.

> Be thee ashamed you neglectful young men, I am ashamed to call you prentices: for how can I call you by that name which you despite. For prentices indeed are those, that betray your practices: such, as being servants know how to obey, that being masters they may be obeyed: for

---

[91]Felix Schelling, *Elizabethan Drama: 1558-1642*, (New York: Russell and Russell, 1935; reprint ed. 1959), p. 183.

[92]Gurr, *The Shakespearean Stage*, p. 50.

[93]T.W. Baldwin, *The Organization and personnel of the Shakespearean Company*, (New York: Russell and Russell, 1961), p. 226.

[94]Peter Moore, *The Apprentice Warningpiece*, (London: 1641), pp. 2-7.

it is as great praise for a subject to obey dutifully, as a Governor to rule well.[95]

Often an actor would solicit for an apprentice. Henslowe wrote that he had bought a boy named James Bristo to act in his company.[96] Actors sometimes acquired several at a time. In spite of the financial aspect of this exchange, they were usually treated as members of the family. They slept in the same rooms as the master's own children and shared the same food. Needless to say, an affection was often kindled between the family and their boarder. Nicholas Tooley, an apprentice who lodged with the Burbages for many years, left the following to his master's wife:

> I do give, unto Mrs. Burbage the wife of my good friend Mr. Cuthbert Burbage (in whose house I now lodge) as a remembrance of my love in respect of her motherly care over me, the sum of L10...[97]

Such testimonials are commonly found among the possessions of the actors during this period. Samuel Gilburn, an actor in Shakespeare's company, remembered his apprentice Augustine Phillips in his will. He left the boy some of his most valuable stage properties. These included his "mouse-colored velvet hose, a white taffety doublet, a black taffety suit, a purple cloak, the sword, dagger and bass viol." Since an actor of the day was partially judged by his wardrobe, these must have been especially welcomed by the young actor.[98]   At least once, the apprentice married into the family of his master. After the death of Richard Burbage, the great actor's apprentice, Dicky Robinson married his wife Winfred Burbage. There would have been at least a sixteen year difference in their ages, but the union must have been very practical for both parties. By marrying Master

---

[95]"A Student's Lamentation that hath sometime been in London an apprentice, for tumults lately in the city happening: for which flue suffered on Thursday the 24 of July last..." (London: William Blackwall, Manuscript from the Folger Library Collection, 1595, pp. 11-12.

[96]Brown, *Shakespeare and the Actors*, pp. 116-119.

[97]Chute, *Shakespeare of London*, p. 161.

[98]Brown, *Shakespeare and the Actors*, p. 115.

Robinson, Mrs. Burbage was assured of keeping her husband's shares in the company. This union represented a sizable financial gain for the young actor.[99]

We can say with some certainty that Shakespeare never had an apprentice. It was necessary that a man have a wife and family before an apprentice was invited into his house. Appearances were important to the Elizabethans, and it would hardly become the reputation of a single man to be living with a young boy. Shakespeare also did not have the space to lodge an apprentice. He was himself a boarder while living in London, and he even may have been an apprentice during his early years in that city.

> Of course, Shakespeare must have been above the regular age for apprentice when he came to London; but in the trades at least it was so much a custom to take grown men as apprentices that regulations had to be made against doing so, especially if the man was married. That there would be nothing peculiar in Shakespeare's becoming an apprentice in the company is shown by the early career of another dramatist, Anthony Munday, which in many respects furnishes a close parallel to that we have supposed for Shakespeare. Munday was apprenticed to John Allde, Stationer, August 24, 1576, for eight years, he being at the time twenty-two or twenty-three. Under our supposition, Shakespeare would have become an apprentice at latest by May, 1587, at the age of twenty-three, for at least the minimum of seven years.[100]

Within the structure of the professional company, Shakespeare could have entered as either an apprentice or as a journeyman. There is some conjecture that his first job may have been to act as a prompter's attendant.[101] It is unlikely that he would have entered the company as an actor unless he had some experience acting in touring companies away from London. Shakespeare encountered a rigid chain of command in the Burbage company; it is safe to say that he started as a journeyman near the bottom of the organizational structure. This novice from Stratford was not about to act with the finest performers of that time until he had

---

[99]Ibid., p. 80.

[100]Baldwin, *The organization of Personnel*, p. 287. There is some discussion of this point among critics. Bradbrook, among others, states that neither Burbage or Shakespeare ever acted as apprentices to any other actor. See: Bradbrook, *The rise of the Common Player*, p. 207.

[101]Baldwin, *The Organization of Personnel*, p. 289.

undergone some sort of apprenticeship program. Apprentice systems were not only a matter of convenience, they were written into the law.

> Even if Richard Burbage probably was not formally apprenticed, still he had received the regular training, and had fulfilled the law concerning apprentices. Also, unless Shakespeare be an exception; no member was drawn from another company before 1603. The presumption from this custom is thus strong that William Shakespeare had gone through the necessary period of training in the company as an actor either as an apprentice or a hired man...In any case, they had served an apprenticeship. This was not only the custom; it was the law.[102]

As previously noted, Richard Burbage, as revealed by his brother, started acting at age thirteen. This was the usual age to begin apprenticeship. He acted under his father at the Theatre Rome, London's first professional playhouse. James Burbage also worked his way up to a management position. His son Cuthbert spoke of his father as "the first builder of playhouses, and was himself in his younger years a player."[103] Ten years after his arrival in London Shakespeare is listed as one of the principle shareholders with Kempe and Burbage. This kind of progression was not unusual. Richard Burbage's apprentice, Nicholas Tooley eventually became a shareholder, and finally a housekeeper of the Globe.[104]

A letter exists from one Master Pyk to his master Edward Alleyn. The writer seems to be a man of good schooling, and he expresses an extreme fondness for the older actor. This was probably the John Pyk who later became a shareholder with the Admiral's Men. In this letter he refers to himself by what seems to be a household nickname, "yor petty pretty pratlyng partying pgy." He was later to use the name John Pig on stage.[105]

---

[102]Ibid., pp. 286-287.

[103]Edwin Nungezer, *A Dictionary of Actors Before 1642*, (New York: Greenwood Press, 1929), p. 67.

[104]Gurr, *The Shakespearean Stage*, p. 26.

[105]Brown, *Shakespeare and the Actors*, p. 114.

The ascension of individual actors up the ranks was an established part of the organization in Elizabethan theatres. In many ways this could be considered a closed system. Rarely did actors from one company cross over to another troupe. Once established the system was self-contained and built a tight ensemble within the ranks of the theatres. Competition among companies was fierce; the apprenticeship program stimulated great loyalty among the individual company members. Since the Theatre started producing plays in 1576, it took about twenty years for the apprentices to become housekeepers: "But the later group, (apprentices) for which we can reasonably assume careful training, does not supply actors to the professional company before 1600."[106] But from the time they entered the company the apprentices were conscious that perseverance could bring them to a position of housekeeper.

The apprenticeship program may have had a chain of progression. As an individual grew older and more experienced he would be cast in more challenging roles and thus take a more prominent position in the company.

> It appears then that each apprentice also had a distinct line, to which he had been specially trained. At graduation of one apprentice, a second was already trained to take his place, and a third was articled to begin his training. This system made it necessary to keep several apprentices.[107]

If Baldwin's conjecture is accurate, boys were sought to fulfill certain needs of the company. A new apprentice would be trained to play a specific type of female character.

> A boy was taken by the member whose duty it was to train a particular line, this line being usually in a general way the female counterpart of his own line as a man. He took the boy of ten and broke him in on minor parts supplied by the dramatist. As the boy grew older, his parts became more difficult till a few years before graduation his master brought in another boy to go through the same process.[108]

---

[106]Beckerman, *Shakespeare at the Globe*, p. 122.

[107]Baldwin, *The Organization of Personnel*, p. 196.

[108]Ibid., p. 26.

If the apprenticeship structure was as elaborate as is suggested, Shakespeare as playwright for the company, would have been under pressure to supply these young actors with parts equivalent to their ability.

> This system of training necessitated the closest cooperation on the part of the dramatist also. It was his business in cooperation with the master to supply proper parts for each youngster to begin with and develop in. He had also to be careful not to create any female part for which there was not a properly trained actor. How intimate this cooperation was may be seen from the fact that in nearly every one of the many specific allusions to the ages of the women, the ages given are not, ideal ages but those of the boys who were to perform the parts.[109]

Shakespeare's plays were the textbooks for the young actors. They were certainly written with specific actors in mind for the major parts, this can not be denied, but in all likelihood he wrote incidental parts for educational purposes.

Beckerman agrees that major actors most likely chose boys who fit their image of themselves, and who could play the type of roles that they had been trained to play:

> Since each of these boys was apprenticed to one of the members of the company, his training and performances would probably have harmonized with adult acting.[110]

What better coach could a young actor have in a specific role than to be tutored by a man who in his younger years had played that same type of character? Making a boy the ward of a musician would not serve the needs of the company, unless he were to become a musician. Baldwin takes this conjecture a step further:

> This principle applies not merely to successions among the major members but also the apprentices from whom the successors to members were to be recruited. These apprentices formed the second most permanent element of the company for long terms, usually about eleven years. It would be natural but not necessary for an apprentice to be trained

---

[109]Ibid., pp. 226-227.

[110]Beckerman, *Shakespeare at the Globe*, p. 134.

up in the line of his master as his possible successor. Thus Pollard, the apprentice to the clown Shank, became himself a clown.[111]

Obviously there were numerous variables which could affect the apprentice order of graduation. Although the maturation process may seem to be beyond the control of the company, the roles of the young actors were not always changed by the onset of puberty.

> The natural transition from playing women to playing men is at the breaking of the voice, but boys' voices broke later in Shakespeare's time than now, and a trained voice not only tends to break later than an untrained one but its alto tone may be prolonged even into its late teens.[112]

This organization probably changed when the companies left London during a plague year; this may have been one of the incentives for the troupes to tour the provinces at the onset of the "black death." There may have been some flexibility in this system:

> The "lead" of the future must be given opportunity to develop as the "juvenile lead" of the present. If the "juvenile lead" does not still develop sufficient dash and adaptability for a "lead," he may still serve a useful function as the important "old man" of the company. The "heavy" of the future must be developed from the "second villain of the present, and so through the successions.[113]

Whether or not this system was strictly adhered to is subject to debate. It does seem reasonable that a permanent company might gravitate to such a structure after only a few years. Theatrical presentation was viewed by the company members as a skill and a trade. Acting techniques had to be passed on to a succeeding generation in order to perpetuate the existence of the professional organization. The intimate contact between the master and his apprentice was the foundation of Elizabethan theatre. The apprentices received an education which

---

[111]Baldwin, *The Organization of Personnel*, pp. 308-309.

[112]Juliet Dusinbere, *Shakespeare and the Nature of Women*, (London: The MacMillan Press, 1975), p. 253. Davies also makes this same point. He maintains that the natural change of the voice can be delayed until the age of seventeen. W. Robertson Davies, *Shakespeare's Boy Actors*, (New York: Russell and Russell, 1964), p. 35.

[113]Baldwin, *The Organization of Personnel*, p. 308.

was perfectly suited to their individual needs. If they acquired the skill and had sufficient perseverance within the system, their rewards were great. William Shakespeare, who left Stratford with very little except possibly a couple of poems in his saddlebags, would return a landed gentleman of considerable wealth.

The specific studies may have been formalized by their masters. The students were trained in many disciplines. In 1616 a book entitled *The Rich Cabinet* furnished with variety of excellent descriptions enumerated the skills which were taught to the apprentices. The list included dancing, singing, music, elocution, a good memory, skill in handling weapons, and "pregnancy of wit." One man probably could not have instructed all of these skills. Other company members may have conducted classes in their precise field of expertise. These lessons may have happened in preparation for a production, but I believe that the chance of extra classes outside regular rehearsals is quite slim. The heavy production schedule must have necessitated that company energy had to be directed towards the mounting the play at hand. T.G., the writer of *The Rich Cabinet*, goes on to note the importance of practice and rehearsal in order to perfect the talents of the young performers.

> ...in all of which he resembleth an excellent spring of water, which grows the more sweeter and the more plentiful by the often drawing out of it: so are all these the more perfect and plausible by the more often practice.[114]

The rehearsal and production schedule must have been grueling. Practice began in the early morning and performances were in the afternoon. Special shows in small indoor theatres like Blackfriars were often requested by the nobility who patronized the professional companies. There was little time for outside education. Plays were given in repertory with new works continually added to the production schedule. As was the case with the adult performers, each boy would have to assume several roles in a single production. Because there are

---

[114]Ivor Brown, *How Shakespeare Spent the Day*, (New York: Hill and Wang, 1962), p. 119.

fewer female roles in Shakespeare's plays, the apprentices were not as taxed as were the major actors.[115] The rehearsals, by necessity, became the primary instructional periods for the apprentices. Shakespeare himself may have played an active role in the training of the young actors. There is evidence that the great playwright may have acted as director for the company. A foreigner visiting England during that period commented that the dramatist played an integral part in the staging of the plays. Johannes Rhenamus wrote:

> ...actors are daily instructed, as it were in school, so that even the most eminent actors have to allow themselves to be taught their places by the dramatists.[116]

This man had obviously witnessed a rehearsal and, if his description is correct, Shakespeare may have been a director in the modern sense. The dramatist may well have blocked the plays and assisted actors with line interpretations. Shakespeare probably had an open script before him and may have made cuttings and corrections during the rehearsal period. Each apprentice would receive coaching on his characterization from the man who wrote the script. One would be hard pressed to imagine a more capable instructor.

Whether the Elizabethan acting style was naturalistic or artificially oratorical is still the subject of much debate. When it comes to the education of the apprentices, the tenets of oratory would be easier for them to acquire.[117] Though indication of emotion could mean the success or failure of an actor's portrayal, they must have received more instruction in the mechanics of delivery: "...their training was not so much in pure acting practice as of rhetoric, specifically pronunciation and gesture."[118] Even if they lacked the ability to clarify motivation, the clarity of their delivery would express the important ideas.

---

[115]Chute, *Shakespeare of London*, pp. 89-92.

[116]Leech, *The Revels History*, p. 113.

[117]Beckerman, *Shakespeare at the Globe*, p. 110.

[118]Gurr, *The Shakespearean Stage*, p. 70.

Instruction in voice and enunciation were started as soon as the apprentice joined the company. This training must have continued until graduation.

The Elizabethan actors probably were concerned with breath control. The delivery of the lines was fairly fast and this necessitated a regularity of breathing. Before the time of Shakespeare, lines were always written with heavy end stops. This enabled the actors to place their breaths at exactly the same place in each line. Lines were delivered fast with plenty of breath to sustain the projection. The effect was, of course, highly artificial. Shakespeare broke away from the regular line scan and heavy end stops. His blank verse demanded even more breath control from the young actors. Lines were longer and punctuation did not always indicate a breathing point for the actors. The placing of breaths in Shakespearean blank verse is difficult for even the experienced actor, requiring hours of coaching in order to master the technique.[119] We must remember, however, that they were working with a more vocally skilled student to begin with. As noted in the first chapter, Elizabethan educational systems developed oral proficiency even before writing. By the time an apprentice joined the company, he had as many as ten years experience in memorization and recitation. The lack of printed materials and the stress on oral skills in public schools may have encouraged the average Elizabethan to be more vocally proficient than those of us who live in the twentieth century. Having worked with children as old as the youngest apprentices, I wonder how the company members found the time to mount such an ambitious performance schedule and coach the young actors in voice.

Nearly all English students of the period were schooled in music as well as oratory. Both public and private schools offered their students instruction in singing and many schools introduced instrumental training at an early age. Even the charity schools, like those located in the London slums of Bridewell, had music classes. Knowledge of music, both theory and practice, would be

---

[119]Chute, *Shakespeare of London*, p. 90.

considered normal for that day. Many of the actors in the company started their careers as itinerant minstrels. Both Kempe and Allyn were accomplished singers and experts at playing the lute.[120] The apprentices were schooled in these skills by some of the finest English performers of that day. Musical instruments were highly valued by the company members and their wills show that they were very happy to leave them to their apprentices.[121]

The apprentices were also taught the dances of the period. Almost all of Shakespeare's comedies include dance. The traditional English dances of the day take great skill and rehearsal in order to perfect their choreography. The boys probably learned such dances as the "galliard" with its intricate footwork, the "capriole" which required "volte" which involved "violently leaping between the steps, and the hurling your partner about the floor."[122] Although most of the dances would have been performed by the adult members of the company, the boys were often called upon to execute elaborate choreography. The dance sequence in *A Midsummer Night's Dream* (II. ii.1) is a perfect example:

> The fairies were all played by children, and their rigid training as dancers must have been useful to them; but Puck, who was not technically a fairy, was played by a grown man.[123]

This dance must have been choreographed by another member of the company; Kempe might have been responsible, since he was famous for his dancing. Even if there were no specific dance classes offered by the company, the apprentices would acquire considerable experience during the rehearsals.

More time was spent drilling the positions used in fencing than any other physical activity. From early in the boy's education, use of weapons and self defense was taught daily. Skill at sword play was a matter of honor for an

---

[120]Ibid., p. 161.
[121]Brown, *Shakespeare and the Actors*, p. 115.
[122]Chute, *Shakespeare of London*, p. 88.
[123]Ibid., p. 178.

Elizabethan gentleman. The audience expected realistic depictions of violence on stage, and the apprentices were carefully trained:

> He had to learn the ruthless technique of Elizabethan fencing. He had to learn how to handle a long, heavy rapier in one hand, with a dagger parrying in the other, and to make a series of savage, calculated thrusts at close quarters from the wrist and forearm, aiming either at his opponents eyes or below the ribs. The actor had to achieve the brutal reality of an actual Elizabethan duel without injuring himself or his opponent, a problem that acquired a high degree of training and of physical coordination.[124]

There are records to evidence that the actors in Shakespeare's company were excellent swordsman. The comic actor, Richard Tarleton, received the "Master of Fence." This was the highest award given by the English fencing schools.[125] It is safe to assume that he passed on that skill to the apprentices under his tutelage.

From all reports the young actors were very successful acting in feminine roles. It may be hard for us to imagine that they could enact the great heroines of Shakespeare's plays as effectively as our modern actresses.[126] Juliet Dusinberre reminds us that we have the opposite problem when we are asked to believe that a girl is masquerading as a boy: "boys make bewitching girls, where women make lumbering youths."[127] We know that the English apprentices spent much time learning how to handle and maintain the elaborate wigs they wore during performance.[128] The Elizabethan audiences seemed to accept boys' impersonations completely. The writer Coryate wrote in his book, *Crudites*

---

[124]Ibid., p. 87.

[125]Ibid., p. 88.

[126]Margaret Webster writes about seeing the boy actors in China portray women. Mei-Lan-Fang, a famous performer of the 1950's, was an extremely graceful and convincing woman. He acted his characters with thoughtful simplicity, and he was especially noted for his seductive roles. The training of Mei-Lan-Fang was done, according to Chinese tradition, exclusively by men. He studied with several elderly actors who had also played women in their younger years. Margaret Webster, *Shakespeare Today*, (London: Dent Publishers, 1957), pp. 20-28.

[127]Dusinberre, *Shakespeare and the Nature of Women*, p. 253.

[128]Baldwin, *The Organization and Personnel*, p. 278.

(1611), how surprised he was to see women on the stage when he visited the continent:

> I saw women act, a thing that I never saw before...and they performed it with as good a grace, action and gesture, and whatsoever convenient for a player, as I ever saw any masculine actor.[129]

Ben Jonson wrote about a famous child star of the day in his play *The Devil is an Ass*. One of his characters comments on one Dicky Robinson's masquerades by calling him "a very pretty fellow" and, "he dresses himself the best, beyond forty of your ladies."[130] Ben Jonson also relates an anecdote about that young performer. One night, as a practical joke, he appeared at a "gossip's feast...dressed like a lawyer's wife." He managed to fool the assembly. Finally, his true identity was revealed to the great amusement of all present. The only comments the ladies could make were to note the taste of the young man's fashions.[131] Another apprentice appeared with the great Richard Burbage on stage in a private performance. John Rice was favorably reviewed: "...two absolute actors, even the verie best our instant time can yield," and was called "a verie faire and beautiful nymph."[132] This same writer witnessed a production of Macbeth which featured John Rice as Lady Macbeth: "A very proper Child well spoken, being clothed like an angel of gladness with a taper of frankincense burning in his hand."[133]

The difference between the apprentices of the professional company and the boy actors in the all-boy companies was one of vocational goals. The apprentices had a stake in the success of their company. Each boy could advance

---

[129]Sir Walter Raleigh, Sir Sidney Lee, and Charles Talbut Onions, eds., *Shakespeare's England: An account of Life and Manners*, (London: Claredon Press, 1962), p. 246. Clifford Leech also reports this encounter: "The general quality of boy actors is suggested by the reaction of an English traveler who saw Venice women playing the parts of women; he remarked in pleased surprise that they were as good as the boys." Leech, *The Revels History of Drama in English*, p. 108.

[130]Brown, *Shakespeare and the Actors*, p. 80.

[131]Raleigh, *Shakespeare's England*, p. 246.

[132]Dennis Bartholomeusz, *Macbeth and the Players*, (London: Cambridge University Press, 1969), p. 11.

[133]Ibid.

eventually to become housekeeper. In the boy companies, a student would remain a student no matter how hard he worked. When he reached the age of sixteen, he graduated leaving his masters and his peers. Having no guarantee of employment, he would be forced to seek out a professional apprenticeship -- something the apprentices in the adult theatres had secured many years before. Boy company members rarely became adult actors.

> Distinction must be made between the boys who played women's parts in the men's companies and the boys who played all the parts at Blackfriars. The former were apprenticed to, and trained by, the men; chosen for their acting ability, although it was an advantage to sing tolerably well, they generally became professional actors when their voices broke. The others were choirboys whose acting might be indifferent, but as singers they were the pick of the country and trained by accomplished musicians.[134]

The boy company members were educated in music and not trained to become professional actors. The goal of one day being a shareholder gave the apprentice, as well as the adult actor, an object for achievement. The boys' association with Shakespeare's troupe made them more than students; it made them professionals.[135]

The organization of the Globe came not from the English academies, but from the crafts guilds. The theatre was founded and supervised not by the "university wits," but by men who had been laborers and guild members themselves. These actors had worked through the system as apprentices, shareholders and housekeepers. Elizabethan theatre was a plebeian enterprize supplying popular drama to the growing ranks of the English middle class; who were themselves guild members. Patronage by the nobility merely sanctified their existence, but Shakespeare and his troupe were dependant on the common people for their livelihood. His plays were written for that "great unwashed" as Edmund Burke would later call them. Their children, and not the children of the nobility,

---

[134]F.E. Halliday, *Shakespeare and His Age*, (New York: Thomas Yoeseloff, 1956), p. 77.
[135]Gurr, *The Shakespearean Stage*, p. 69.

became the acting apprentices. The organization of the English theatre evolved from the medieval tradition of the guild; from this system of one to one instruction it drew its strength.

> It was with this apprentice element that the playwright would have the most serious problems. He was obliged by dramatic custom to use these apprentices to represent women, and he must have some principle women in his play, 'For what's a play without a woman in it?' But these boys, like all others, had the disconcerting habit of growing up, changing in physical and mental characteristics and capabilities even from play to play. It was almost as if a sculptor had to express himself in perishable clay. Therefore the dramatist had to provide a simple part to begin with and gradually to increase the part in difficulty till the pupil was finally the master in his art and quality. Then the apprentice graduated and the playwright-school teacher had the whole process to repeat with the next pupil.[136]

We must remember that Shakespeare's company often repeated his more popular plays. Baldwin's notion that the writing of scripts was systematized to accommodate the educational needs of the apprentices is exaggerated at best. It is highly improbable that Shakespeare developed a whole new set of plays for each group of apprentices. I can only suggest that the needs of the young actors probably affected the writing of scripts during his nineteen or twenty year theatrical career. Since we know that he wrote major parts with Burbage in mind, it is safe to infer that he created individual women's roles for the apprentices.

Shakespeare's company was a small and closely knit unit in a plutocratic society. His plays were constructed expressly for his troupe. He knew the talents and limitations of each apprentice and penned the characters accordingly: "These parts were written to be acted by boys...,"[137] At first glance, the structure of the troupe might seem to be a limiting force on the artistic expression of the

---

[136]Baldwin is guilty of forcing his research to corroborate his thesis. Although his conclusions are conjectures and often inaccurate, his book remains one of the few works which attempts to align individual actors with major roles. His study is outdated, and further research must be made into this controversial area. Computers might assist academicians in matching characters to actors, and thus more accurately evaluate the educational processes associated with the apprentices. Baldwin, *The Organization of Personnel of the Shakespearean Company*, p. 319.

[137]Davies, *Shakespeare's Boy Actors*, p. 3.

playwright. Surely he was forced to keep the physical expression of love to a minimum.[138] But in his writing of the female roles, the poetry expresses all the character innuendo the young actors might only be able to indicate. "...the dominating characteristic of them all is their superabundant femininity...,"[139] With equal ease Shakespeare created boyish heroines for many of his comedies. His girls could slip into a doublet and hose as simply as they could don a farthingale.

> The boy actors prompted the creation of boyish heroines. Disguise freed the dramatist to explore,...Moore would have approved of Shakespeare's suggestion that the masculine spirit makes a woman not less but more feminine.[140]

Were the great female roles out of the apprentices' range? Critics have debated this point for centuries. It has been noted that many of the characters seem to be written for one taller and more mature boy with a younger boy usually playing that character's confidant. (Desdemona and Emilia are exceptions to this.) We can easily imagine these light comic parts played by young men.[141] But how could a mere child play Lady Macbeth or Cleopatra? As previously noted, John Rice played the first role with considerable success. He was certainly no child when he acted this mature queen. He may have been in his early twenties, but he helped the play to have a considerable run at the Globe. Cleopatra, the aging Queen, appears beyond the abilities of even an older apprentice. She has more lines than any other female character and is judged by many to be Shakespeare's most complex heroine. Davies decided that this could be played by a sixteen-year-old apprentice. He maintains that the part would be approached from a station of aloof dignity and that her less than regal moments would be suggested by the lines.[142] Brown argues this point. He believes the part too great for any boy

---

[138]Chute, *Shakespeare of London*, p. 160.

[139]Davies, *Shakespeare's Boy Actors*, p. 1.

[140]Dusinberre, *Shakespeare and the Nature of Women*, p. 271.

[141]Leech, *The Revels History*, p. 108.

[142]Davies, *Shakespeare's Boy Actors*, pp. 132-133.

actor. As proof he cites its apparent failure on the Elizabethan stage. Little evidence of production exits today. If it ever became part of the repertory, it was dropped quickly. John Dryden's popular play on the same subject may have kept it off the boards. Not until the nineteenth century was it produced with any regularity. Brown blames the young actor for the failure of this ambitious work.[143]

The fact remains, Shakespeare wrote for these apprentices. With their constant changing of identities, his comedies exploit the potential of the young actors. "The boy actor is an instrument, and Shakespeare uses him with the sense of his possibilities and limits,..."[144] The apprentices gave Shakespeare the freedom to express women of all ages and social standings. These boys were not limited by the Elizabethan notions of how a woman must act; they expressed femininity in a naive and completely human way. "Disguise draws men and women together in the comedies through their discovery of the artifice of difference which social custom sustains."[145] With this confusion of sexual identities, Shakespeare exposes one of his primary themes: "Shakespeare believed that for a man to be more than a boy, as for a woman to be more than a child, the masculine and feminine must marry in spirit."[146] His characters were written to emphasize their humanity, not their sexuality. Some of the mature female characters such as Cleopatra and Cressida are obvious exceptions to this contention. Writing for boy actors permitted the Bard more freedom of expression. These boys were allowed to do what Elizabethan women could not. Their characters emerged as freer, more independent women released from societal expectations. If Shakespeare was a feminist, he acquired a vehicle for expression through the use of the boy actors. Perhaps, as the foremost teacher of the apprentices, Shakespeare felt a social responsibility to educate them morally

---

[143]Brown, *Shakespeare and the Actors*, p. 109.

[144]Dusinberre, *Shakespeare and the Nature of Women*, p. 269.

[145]Ibid., p. 265.

[146]Ibid., p. 291.

as well as professionally. His scripts were their textbooks, and his value of life and humanity became their most important lesson.

CHAPTER III

THE ELIZABETHAN BOY COMPANIES:

THEIR EDUCATION AND PERFORMANCE EXPERIENCE

The tradition of performances by boy actors extends throughout the Middle

Ages. Usually the productions were associated with some seasonal celebration:

> During the late Middle Ages and Renaissance, children's
> performances, generally of high quality, were usually part of an elaborate
> program of seasonal entertainment, a ritual of festivity, a blaze of revelry
> against the midwinter gloom.[147]

There are records of productions done at the Chapel of St. Paul's as early

as 1378. The performances may have arisen as an extension of a certain winter

feast. This celebration was known as the Festival of the Boy Bishops. This was

a day of masquerading and foolery. The high point of the feast was a processional

of the choirboys dressed in the robes of the high priests. Often these youngsters

would assume the duties of their elders and exercise their power in mock

seriousness. Impersonations and parody must have played a large part in the

entertainment.[148] Although probably not a scripted dramatic event, the evening

appearance of the boys at the Feast of the Holy Innocents contained many of the

elements later found in the productions of the professional boy companies. These

ceremonies were discontinued before the sixteenth century. The church leaders

may have been offended by the young actors' disguises. Often their portrayals

bordered on the obscene. Although the audiences loved them, they were stopped

by order of the church officials.

---

[147]Michael Shapiro, *Children of Revels: The Boy Companies of Shakespeare's Time and Their Plays*, (New York: Columbia University Press, 1977), p. 31.

[148]Bradbrook, *The Rise of the Common Player*, p. 215.

Shapiro, on the other hand, believes that there may have been little connection between this mid-winter festival and the formation of the professional boy companies.

> True theatrical-performances by the choirboys arise not from the ceremony of the Boy Bishop, but from tropes introduced into the Mass after the ninth century.[149]

Early records show that performances given by the boys of Saint Paul's were not comedies or masquerades; rather they were serious interpretations of biblical stories integrated into a formal worship service. Only later did they become primarily comic.[150]

Many of the early dramatic presentations were associated with private chapels constructed by the nobility for members of their immediate family.

> During the late Middle Ages and Early Renaissance, European sovereigns and nobles of every degree maintained chapels for their personal worship, which they staffed as well as their taste and vanity urged and their resources allowed.[151]

Another theory is suggested by the compilers of an early account of Shakespeare's life.

> The formation of these companies was obviously a development of the stage convention by which in Shakespeare's day the parts of women were played by boys.[152]

Shapiro's theory may be inaccurate. Although the tradition boys playing women's roles was used in the traveling adult companies and regional festivals, the permanent adult professional theatres reached popularity after the boys' companies. Probably, the tradition of female impersonation by the child actors influenced the casting of the professional adult companies. The precedent of using boys as women was established in the plays by the choirboys and the Elizabethan audiences expected this convention when they attended the first professional

---

[149]Shapiro, *Children of Revels*, p. 9.

[150]Bradbrook, *The Rise of the Common Player*, p. 215.

[151]Shapiro, *Children of Revels*, p. 6.

[152]Raleigh et al., *Shakespeare's England*, p. 246.

productions by adults. The men may have even borrowed actors from St. Paul's for their early productions:

> In the early part of Elizabeth's reign, men and boys' troupes had sometimes acted together for a court performance, for at this time men had few apprentices...As they established themselves, and acquired their boy actors, the need for collaboration vanished.[153]

Clearly, many of the practices of the professional companies were drawn from the traditions of the boy choirs and their performances and the professional touring companies.

The greatest rival of the Children of St. Paul's was the company known as the Children of the Chapel Royal. Their first performance was not until 1506, but they became popular very quickly. By 1528 they were performing before Henry VIII.[154] The organization of the personnel was similar to that of St. Paul's. The company itself consisted of twelve choirboys. One deacon usually headed the troupe and acted as master and teacher to the boys. Two musicians were hired to supply the accompaniment for the singing and the numerous dances. In addition there were three servants, usually including at least one elderly woman to act as cook and nursemaid, another would act as a teacher to round out their education.[155]

The boys' popularity with the nobility insured their existence. In the eighteen years before the first theatre was built by James Burbage in 1576, there were seventy-eight performances in the royal court. Thirty-two were staged by adults, but the boy companies appeared forty-six times. As the most popular company, the Children of St. Paul's performed before the royal court twenty-one times.[156] The Revels Account indicates that child troupes entertained at more than sixty individual performances. Often their appearance was a yearly

---

[153]Bradbrook, *The Rise of the Common Player*, p.234.

[154]Schelling, *Elizabethan Drama*, p. 111.

[155]Since there were women on the staff of the choirboys' organization, it is possible that they assisted the master in coaching the young actors in feminine deportment. Halliday, *Shakespeare and His Age*, p. 50.

[156]Ibid., p. 49.

occurrence. These court ordered shows were in addition to their regular public productions. The nobility viewed them at night, and this meant that the boys worked long hours on court ordered days.[157]

In order to compete with the adult professional theatres, the children's companies established afternoon production schedules. The regular performance time was about four o'clock in the afternoon, the shows lasted until well after six o'clock.[158] Early in their development the productions were free to all who cared to attend. Often they were associated with a worship service and they were supported by donations from the parishioners. Eventually a fee was charged at the door and this began a trend toward commercialization. Wescote, an early choirmaster, mentions in his will "one Shepherd that keepeth the door of plays."[159] This indicates there was a charge to the public.

As the boys became more popular, the choirmaster tried to maintain the original intention of the organization:

> Despite this drift toward commercialization they continued to style themselves as choirboy troupes,...in order to foster the illusion that they were amateur children's troupes, the traditional purveyors of dramatic entertainment to the court.[160]

This illusion of amateurism also served to reduce the criticism from the community. As many educators will attest, amateur children's productions are often accepted by otherwise highly critical audiences because they are expected to be less than professional.

The boys were more than apprentices, they were wards to the choirmaster. This meant that they acted according to his will. He literally possessed them as if they were property. He was obligated to feed and clothe them. In addition he assumed responsibility for their education and moral instruction. The records of the Chapel Royal show purchases of bread, ale and candles among other things,

---

[157]Shelling, *Elizabethan Drama*, p. 117.
[158]Bradbrook, *The Rise of the Common Player*, p. 218.
[159]Shapiro, *Children of Revels*, p. 13.
[160]Ibid., p. 1.

which were obtained by the master for his boys.[161] There were only a few rules which the headmaster was obliged to follow.

> Farrants' (Headmaster of the Chapel Royal) indentures for the Mastership of Windsor stipulated that he should leave the boys as well clothed as he found them; but rich vestments in the choir and rags in their schoolroom were probably the choristers' lot.[162]

The masters were originally employed as instructors of voice. But as the boys' companies became more popular the role of the leader was expanded. Nicholas Udall was the first to use the boys as an acting troupe. Although not really associated with the choir, he cultivated royal taste by presenting a boys' production of a play by Plautus. This English version was said to have been a great success, and he was subsequently asked to return. Udall was head of Westminster in 1552, but his activity in theatre spans the years 1534 to 1541.[163] He worked primarily as an administrator during his later years.

Richard Edwards became the master of the Chapel Children in 1561 and encouraged the production of non-religious plays. He was also a playwright for the boys. One of his plays, *Damon and Pythias*, has survived.[164] The first headmaster to organize the boys into a professional dramatic company was Edward's successor William Cornish. He also wrote his own plays and met considerable success during his lifetime. His works were called "most magnificent court entertainments" and the resulting royal patronage stimulated the popularity of the young company.[165] Cornish was perhaps the first headmaster to place equal emphasis on music and drama. He often acted in his own plays with the boys. He appeared as Calchas when Chapel Royal produced *Troilus and Cirseyde*.[166]

---

[161]Bradbrook, *The Rise of the Common Player*, p. 221.
[162]Ibid., p. 220.
[163]Schelling, *Elizabethan Drama*, p. 111.
[164]Shapiro, *Children of Revels*, p. 7.
[165]Bradbrook, *The Rise of the Common Player*, p. 29.
[166]Shapiro, *Children of Revels*, p. 219.

The rise of the Children of St. Paul's is credited to two early masters, John Redford and Sebastian Westcott. Westcott was the first choirmaster to instruct both singing and acting. He actively recruited noted writers to write scripts for the boys' performances. The famous interlude writer, John Heywood, became very successful working for the Children of St. Paul's.[167] Richard Mulcaster took over this company in 1600 and revived the popularity of the boy actors. He defended theatre against the rising criticisms from the Puritans. He was said to be "the enthusiastic believer in the drama as a means of teaching boys good behavior and audacity."[168]

As the boy companies became professional, the role of the choirmaster shifted from that of a teacher to one of a theatrical manager. The first to exploit the business opportunities involved with the success of this genre was Richard Farrant. In 1576 he leased a building from Sir William Moore. This structure became Blackfriars Theatre and would be the home of the newly organized Chapel Children. Theatre was not viewed favorably by many segments of English society, and there is some evidence that Sir William Moore did not realize Farrant's intention when granting him the lease. Moore wrote, "Farrant pretended unto me to use the house only for the teaching of Children of the Chapel but made it a continual house for plays."[169] An original letter from Farrant found in the Folger Library, bears out Moore's testimony that he knew little about the new use of his property at Blackfriars. In this letter Farrant requests permission to renovate the space. He wanted to "pull downe one partition and so make two rooms one."[170] Nowhere in the letter does he mention a reason for this change. This one large room was to become the main hall for the new theatre. Although Moore may have been against the establishment of the new theatre, he took no

---

[167]Halliday, *Shakespeare and His Age*, p. 49.

[168]Ibid., p. 223.

[169]Shapiro, *Children of Revels*, p. 14.

[170]Richard Farrant, Autographed letter sighed to William Moore, London, August 27, 1574. Folger Library Special Collection.

action to prevent it from opening. Since admission was charged; more than likely, Moore was happy to have a successful paying tenant in his building.[171] The patent from the royal family made Farrant's business legal and the children continued production until 1584.[172]

Although Farrant was noted for being a shrewd business man, most choirmasters never became wealthy working with the boy companies. A headmaster named Hunnis complained in 1583 that all those he had known died in debt.[173] That year he filed a petition to the Queen to increase the yearly allotment for the company. At that time he was given forty pounds a year to support himself, twelve children, an usher and "a woman to keep them clean."[174] This amount was about ten times what a London schoolmaster of this period would be making for a year's work. Also, the choirmaster had access to other capital. He was usually paid ten pounds to stage a production in the court. Performances yielded substantial box office receipts and much of this money went into the pocket of the company manager. Although a choirmaster's overhead must have been high, he could not be considered financially poor.

It took a unique talent to manage a children's company:

> Multifarious, indeed, must have been the duties of a royal choirmaster in those days, for not only must he have been a Doctor of Music to drill and to lead his choir in church and perhaps accompany them on the organ, but it was likewise his duty to devise new sacred music and secular songs, to invent pageants and shows, to write plays, and to teach his young charges how to act them to the satisfaction of the Queen and a critical court.[175]

---

[171]Leech, *The Revels History of Drama in English*, p. 109.

[172]There is an excellent copy of a boys' company patent in the Folger Library. It gives permission to Her Majesty's Children "to use and exercise the arts and quality of playing comedies, histories, Interludes, Morales, Pastorals, Stageplays and other such like they have studied..." Patent roll 1613 copied 1880. Halliwell-Phillips Scrapbooks, Vol. "Children's Companies," p. 134. Folger Library Special Collection.

[173]Bradbrook, *The Rise of the Common Player*, p. 226.

[174]Schelling, *Elizabethan Drama*, p. 115.

[175]Whitaker, *Shakespeare's Use of Learning*, p. 14.

After considering the amount of rehearsal time it must have taken to produce their large repertory of plays, one wonders if there was any time left for education. There are some indications that the choirmaster may have recruited others to help educate his wards: "Sometimes a poet, sometimes an old player would join, and start training the boys."[176] As the masters of the apprentices were responsible for the education of their wards, so the choirmaster educated the boys. These boys, however, had even fewer rights than their counterparts in the professional companies: "...choristers were treated as chattels of their master, having none of the safe guards of prentices, although their education was entirely vocational."[177] Of course the children were much younger than the apprentices in general, but they were about the same age as the apprentices in the adult theatre companies. The boys entered the choir at the age of seven or eight and would remain until the age of thirteen or fourteen.[178] The major difference between the boys and the apprentices, however, was that the children continued their education through the church school. They were considered students who were under the control of the master. English books on education during that period gave the teachers the same authority as parents to administer corporal punishment.[179]

The Queen's warrant of 1585 sets down the basic guidelines for the education of the choirboys: "to take up such apt and meet children as are most fit to be instructed and framed in the art and science of music and singing."[180] Singing was the original intention for their organization, but as their dramatic productions became more and more popular, their musical education lost much of its focus. The boys received a secular education at the Chapel grammar school, but there was always a clear distinction made between the grammar students and

---

[176]Schelling, *Elizabethan Drama*, p. 112.

[177]Bradbrook, *The Rise of the Common Player*, p. 220.

[178]Shapiro, *Children of Revels*, p. 8.

[179]William Kemp, *The Education of Children in Learning*, (London: Thomas Orwin, 1588), Folger Library Special Collection, p. 8.

[180]Schelling, *Elizabethan Drama*, p. 116.

the choristers. Rarely did the students mix socially. "...their school (choirboys'), when alluded to at all, was called the song school to distinguish it from the grammar school."[181]

The grammar school associated with a chapel was an extension of a medieval system of education in which the royalty sent their children to the clergy for instruction. The chapel grammar schools offered an education specially designed for the elite. Aside from a stress on manners and deportment, church schools included more education in the arts.[182] Musical training became an important part of the daily lessons. Also, unlike the public schools, these grammar schools taught and practiced drama and studied dramatic literature. The reading of Terence in the original Latin was recommended to improve a student's proficiency at verbal skills.

Often these chapel schools produced their own plays for public performance. "It may be that throughout the Middle Ages grammar school boys were more active in dramatic representation than choirboys."[183] During the Middle Ages the primary task of the choirboys was to sing in the church choir. The move into professional theatre came relatively late in their evolution. As the boys' choirs became popular, the productions of the grammar schools all but disappeared:

> Meanwhile, the drama of the schools, so venturous and experimental in the first half of the century, declined and withered away to Christmas shows and other subdramatic forms.[184]

With the closing of the theatres in 1642, drama was all but removed from both the public schools and the chapel schools. Dramatic production was exclusively

---

[181]Harold Newcombe Hillebrand, *The Children Actors*, (New York: Russell and Russell, 1964), p. 106.

[182]There is an excellent treatise on the education of children of the nobility to be found in the Folger Library. It is very specific about the necessity of an artistically oriented education for the elite. John Jones, *The Arts and Science of Perfering Bodie and Soule in al Health, Wisdom, and Catholic Religion*, (London: Ralph Newberrie, 1579), Folger Library Special Collection, p. 13.

[183]Hillebrand, *The Child Actors*, p. 10.

[184]Bradbrook, *The Rise of the Common Player*, p. 50.

reserved for the boy companies which had become a popular professional entertainment.

For the children of the grammar school, music study occupied only a short period of each school day, but for the choristers most of their education involved music theory and practice:

> The choir schools provided an excellent musical education, which included instruction in polyphonic singing and playing such instruments as organ, virginals, viols, cornets and recorders.[185]

Each student was expected to master various skills. The choirboys were often called upon to play the accompaniment during the productions. Frequently boys were encouraged to take up an instrument when their lack of vocal skill prevented them from participating in the choir. In 1606, Alice Cook signed an indenture agreement with the management at Blackfriars. For a period of three years her son was to be trained in performance techniques. "...to practice and exercise the quality of playing."[186] As the company became more professional, the notions of education and royal service began to be replaced by a kind of guild apprentice system. This indenture indicates that Blackfriars was more than just a school: its professional status had elevated the organization to a business. During the late 1500's Blackfriars entered into the same contractual agreements as the other professional guilds.

The boys in the company fulfilled three distinct functions. Although the services needed changing according to the production requirements, individual boys were usually trained to perform only one of the following functions. First there were the actors. These were usually the more experienced boys in the company who were able to handle the long monologues required in Elizabethan drama. Often these principal young actors would play the leads in several of the plays in repertory. The speaking parts would not always fall to the older boys. Part of the charm of the child players depended upon the comic effect displayed

---

[185]Shapiro, *Children of Revels*, p. 8.
[186]Bradbrook, *The Rise of the Common Player*, p. 240.

when a very young boy acted the part of an old man. The second function was filled by those students who were more proficient at musical skills. They either sang in the choir during the interludes or played an instrument to accompany the ballads and numerous dances. Finally were the silent participants who were dressed in costume: much of the appeal of these productions depended on the spectacle of large crowd scenes with sumptuous costume and scenic effects.[187] The children were often dressed in royal livery while on stage. Many of the costumes were donated to the company by their royal patrons and then cut to the size of the young actors.[188]

At one time the Children of the Chapel Royal were housed in the rooms adjoining the theatre, but the boys' companies were not the only ones to use the Blackfriars for rehearsals and performance space. Once the theatre became a popular enterprise, the Gentlemen of the Chapel and other professional dramatic companies used the house during the off-season. Often smaller private performances were staged in this more intimate theatre. Shakespeare's company utilized Blackfriars for its winter productions.

Discipline at Blackfriars was strict and the boys gave evidence of living up to the expectations of their young age. Some of the boys' rooms were later rented to the Lord Chamberlain who complained in a letter that the choristers had "cut up the lead roof with pen knives and bored it with bodkins until it leaked."[189] Again the headmaster was asked to assume the cost of repairs. The relations between the professional adults and the boys remained strained, to say the least.

Since Blackfriars was a smaller theatre and there was no pit and only limited seating, its admission prices were considerably higher than the larger outdoor theatres such as the Globe. It obviously attracted an elite and educated

---

[187]Hillebrand, *Child Actors*, p. 29.
[188]Bradbrook, *The Rise of the Common Player*, p. 225.
[189]Bradbrook, *The Rise of the Common Player*, p. 225.

audiences who were quite articulate in recording their reactions to the young performers. The comments on the choirboys' acting and singing abilities are profuse. Although Shakespeare did not admire their talents, there were many who did respect them. One foreign visitor to sixteenth century London felt that the singing of the choirboys was only surpassed by the nuns of Milan.[190] Their acting also drew praise and a faithful following for many years. When Nathaniel Giles took over the theatre in 1597, he recruited many of the finest young talents of his day. The plays produced by this company were to elicit great enthusiasm from critics and public alike.

Perhaps the most famous name to emerge during these years was that of Nathan Fields.

> Nathan Fields was Jonson's favorite, "his scholar", for, when he was pressed for service with the Chapel, Jonson took his education in hand, and read him the satires of Horace and some of the epigrams of Martial -- not, perhaps, reading that we should choose today for a boy of nine.[191]

Though Nathan was a member of the choirboys, he received from Ben Johnson the kind of education that an apprentice might get from his master. We have no records to indicate how thorough this education was, but we do know that the two were dedicated to each other. Although Fields probably went against the wishes of his father, a Puritan Minister, he became a great success in theatre.[192] He later moved from the Chapel Royal to become a member of Shakespeare's company. Several years after joining their ranks, he became a shareholder. He was one of the few child actors to receive billing in both the boys companies and then later the adult companies.[193]

---

[190] M.M. Reese, *Shakespeare and His World and Work*, (New York: St. Martin's Press., Inc., 1953), p. 22.

[191] Halliday, *Shakespeare and His Age*, p. 225.

[192] Raleigh et. al., *Shakespeare's England*, p. 245.

[193] The Halliwell-Phillips scrapbooks contain many well preserved handbills from the children and adult companies. Folger Library Special Collection.

The Halliwell-Phillips collection at the Folger Library includes a poem which is attributed to Nathan Fields. This work discusses acting in very intelligent terms.

> But let Art look in truth, she like a mirror
> Reflect her comfort, ignorances, or sits in her owne brow,
> Being made afraid of her unnatural complexion
> As ugly women (when they are araid by glasses)
> Loath their truer Reflection,
> Then how can such opinions injure thee,
> That trouble at their own deformity?[194]

These words illustrate that Fields thought seriously about his art. He echoes the words of Shakespeare when he demands reality and honesty in his craft. If these words are indeed from the pen of this great child actor, then Jonson's tutoring must have been more than learning by rote.

The strength of the apprentice system was the personal contact between student and master. This type of individualized education could not possibly be done by the choirmaster with his numerous administrative obligations. For Fields, conceptual and practical education must have come from Jonson. As previously noted, very few of the choirboys actually crossed over to become professional actors in the adult companies. Fields is one notable exception. He went on to become one of the most popular actors of this period and was particularly noted for his heroic leads. Without a doubt, Jonson must have contributed to Fields' mastery of his craft and his success on the stage.

It may be that Jonson's interest in young Fields was not unique. It is known that he established a friendship and admiration with another important child actor, Solomon Pavy. Pavy died at a very early age, and Jonson's epitaph to the boy is a touching admiration of the loss of a fine talent.

> Years he numbered scarce thirteen
>   When Fates turned cruel,
> Yet three filled zodiacs had he been

---

[194]This excerpt is from an original undated handbill fixed with the name "Nat. Fields" Halliwell-Phillips Scrapbooks, vol. "Minor Actors," p. 75. Folger Library Special Collection.

> The stages jewel;
> And did act, what now we moan
> Old men so duly
> As sooth, the Parcae thought him one,
> He played so truly.[195]

When addressing the dramatic education of the boys, scholars are forced to make conjectures about the style of Elizabethan acting. Was recitation enough for the young actors, or did the audiences expect a more realistic interpretation of character? Michael Shapiro believes that assigning a single style to the acting in the boys' companies could limit our understanding of their performances.

> Unfortunately, most writers on the subject...argue over whether the prevailing acting style for all actors in the period -- children and adults -- was "natural" or "formal," terms which are vague, imprecise and wrongly thought to be mutually exclusive.[196]

Shapiro suggests that their style changed with the demands of each production, since many of their plays forced the young actors to imitate famous adults. When acting the parts of living royalty the boys must have adopted a lofty style. As noted in Jonson's epitaph for Pavy, their acting could be remarkably realistic, but because their plays depended on parody for laughs, most of it was probably artificial, over-blown and "hammy".

The content of the plays illustrates the demands placed upon the young actors. The scripts were originally used to supplement the boys' education, and for a long time they contained much that could be considered academic and theoretical: "...the plays were often debates of scholastic questions which elsewhere the students might tackle in all solemnity."[197] These works were written to complement the boys' performance strengths.

> Plays written for the children's company do not require much emotional depth, and playwrights sometimes exploit the childishness of the actors for ironic effect; but within these limits even the children were required to display a wide stylistic range, from the declamatory to the

---

[195]Halliday, *Shakespeare and His Age*, p. 77.

[196]Shapiro, *Children of Revels*, p. 113.

[197]Bradbrook, *The Rise of the Common Player*, p. 29.

colloquial. And the theatre itself could be as much a factor as the play: there is evidence that once the adult companies had the experience of playing in small private houses as well as large public ones, they developed a quieter style for the former.[198]

Various types of plays were produced by the children's companies. Often lavish masques and costume displays were requested by the nobility. The most popular theme involved knights and battles with mythic monsters. These programs complimented the elite by pointing up their heroic ancestry. Many plays were written like the moralities which were popular in a preceding period. The plays written in this form were always secular and usually bawdy. John Marston wrote for the boys' companies early in his career. His *Histriomastix or the Player Whipped* was a play written after the model of the English morality. It included such symbolic characters as Sluttishness, Bondage and Poverty.[199] Ancient fables were another popular source for these plays. Usually they were presented seriously, but often were satirized by the young actors. The myths of Ulysses, Pompey and Ajax were parodied. Contemporary English comedies played well before the elite and the lower classes. Some of the most popular were *Six Fools*, *Jack and Gill*, and *The History of Error*.[200] Often the royalty requested plays on certain themes. Once the boys of St. Paul were ordered by the throne to perform a play against the "heretic Martin Luther" for the benefit of the French ambassador.[201]

There seemed to be no social stigma for a playwright to work exclusively for the boys' companies, they attracted some of the finest writers of that generation. Famous writers were attracted to the children's companies for many reasons. First, they usually were paid more for their scripts than their counterparts in the professional adult troupes. "For in 1600,...the professional

---

[198]Leech, *The Revels History of Drama in English*, p. 116.

[199]G.B. Harrison, *Elizabethan Plays and Players*, (Ann Arbor, Michigan: The University of Michigan Press, 1956), p. 207.

[200]The latter play may have been used as source for Shakespeare's *Comedy of Errors*. Schelling, *Elizabethan Drama*, p. 117.

[201]Bradbrook, *The Rise of the Common Player*, p. 32.

theatre was primarily an actor's theatre, run by actors for the profit of actors."[202] Second, unless the playwright became personally involved with the production of his own plays, the actors felt they had the right to change or abridge them. Often what ended up on the boards was far removed from the playwright's original manuscript; the actors ignored the poetry of the writing, and even Shakespeare complained that many comics adopted the detestable practice of adlibbing on stage. The boy actors on the other hand, took orders and probably recited the playwright's lines as written. Third, because they were children their words seemed more innocent even if they were slanderous. This allowed the individual playwright more freedom of expression. Toward the end of the sixteenth century the boys became a mouthpiece for the playwright. If the adult companies were indeed actors' theatres, then the boys' companies were playwright's theatres.

John Lyly was a notable example. His first play was staged by the Children of St. Paul's in 1580 and this began a long association between them. Unfortunately, the Children of St. Paul's was ordered to cease production in 1591, at the height of Lyly's talents, and for eight years their theatre remained dark. This closing encouraged the popularity of Shakespeare's company, but Lily never again regained his former prominence.[203] Many of Lyly's early plays were staged in the medieval tradition. For example, *Campaspe* was staged before the Queen in 1584. It was constructed of short scenes in the old morality play form. Each scene was housed in a separate mansion.[204] His plays are filled with wit and frequently use wordplay to generate humor. "It is commonly believed that his emphasis on verbal cleverness rather than deep feeling reflects the abilities, and limits, of the children."[205] Lyly used dramatic allegory as a means of social criticism. Often his political stand in these plays made him

---

[202]Reese, *Shakespeare and His World and Work*, p. 222.

[203]Schelling, *Elizabethan Drama*, p. 125.

[204]Harrison, *Elizabethan Plays and Players*, p. 26.

[205]Leech, *The Revels History of Drama in English*, p. 110.

unpopular with the ruling class. In spite of the content of his dramas, the nobility continued to flock to the theatre. Perhaps they were tantalized by hearing criticism of their peers. In *Endimion, the Man in the Moon*, Lyly clearly alludes to the imprisonment and execution of Mary of Scotland. This was an especially dangerous topic during these times.[206]

The writers not only took risks and poked fun at the ruling classes, but they teased their competitors. Many plays contained gibes aimed at other popular writers of the period. One reason that these plays are not revived today is that they contain so many contemporary allusions that are incomprehensible to modern audiences. Through the end of the century the content of the Chapel productions became more satirical. As the novelty of children playing adults began to wear off, the masters and playwrights searched for new ways to entertain their elite clientele.

> ...adult companies in public theatre offered healthy, moral, good-tempered plays, while the boys' companies specialized in mocking and salacious satire, much of it directed against the middle class.[207]

The English middle class, which had grown so prosperous and powerful during the sixteenth century, was threatening the security of the monarchial system. The adult companies catered to all segments of London society: Shakespeare's plays were written for the pit as much as the boxes. In the boys' companies the audience had to be acknowledged constantly. True, they came to see the production, but they also came to be seen.

> In Blackfriars or St. Paul's, boy actors could provide a school of compliment, a gossip shop, an opportunity for the audience to display fine clothes, nice judgement, lofty pretensions.[208]

These plays always included long speeches of praise contrasted with ridicule against the lower segments of English society. But within these rather narrow

---

[206]Schelling, *Elizabethan Drama*, p. 130.
[207]Leech, *The Revels History of Drama in English*, p. 98.
[208]Bradbrook, *The Rise of the Common Player*, p. 231.

limits, the playwrights perfected a popular and relatively artistic means of expression.

> The genius of the childrens' plays was to reassure the spectator that he had achieved his own wishful view of himself by encouraging him to identify with attractive characters of high rank, and to scatter his doubts about his social status by inviting him to ridicule "others." ...Praise of individuals was a time-honored method of teaching virtue through examples.[209]

The acting on stage was the last thing that concerned this self-centered audience. In fact a serious attempt at an emotional display might shift the attention away from those sitting in the small, well-lit auditorium.

> The actors are but instruments or toys by which the audience conducts their own "dalliance" and children were better suited for this game than men actors,...[210]

The playwrights took every chance to emphasize that their actors had not reached maturity. Often they wrote parts for adult actors in the children's plays. Having a man on stage with these small, masquerading boys heightened the comedy while flattering the audience's intelligence. Constant self-reference kept the audience conscious that they were witnessing parody and not reality. But the most popular and dangerous technique was the use of bawdry. The plays of this genre abounded with sexual puns and slurs. Many of the gags alluded to the sexual impotence of children who tried so hard to act adult.[211] Their upper class audience found such ideas hilarious and encouraged the inclusion of more bawdry in the plays of the early seventeenth century. The scripts reduced their emphasis on social criticism and evolved a form which mixed ridicule and sexual innuendo. Dekker and Webster were later to exploit the unchanging formulas of the bedroom farce. It will be remembered that these same elements of parody and ridicule had undergone a similar development in the Festival of the Boy Bishop. This festival degenerated into a community attack: insults and obscenities directed

---

[209]Shapiro, *Children of Revels*, p. 104.

[210]Bradbrook, *The Rise of the Common Player*, p. 232.

[211]Shapiro, *Children of Revels*, p. 105.

toward the church hierarchy. Years before the evolution of the boys' companies the celebration was discontinued. A similar fate awaited the dramatic productions of the children's choirs.

From their inception these productions were the subject of vigorous attacks from the pulpit and from government officials. Mandates were issued against John Lyly's plays. In 1584 the Privy Council appealed for censorship of the boys' companies.

> ...the players take upon themselves to handle in their plays certain masters of Divinity and of State unfit to be suffered.[212]

This was the first of a series of accusations against Lyly. His theatre would remain open until 1590. The details of closing his theatre in 1590 are still sketchy, but we can assume that the throne was increasingly disturbed by the content of the productions and removed the royal patent. All children's companies of London were inactive through the next decade. During these years the professional adult companies prospered, partially because the nobility had returned to the popular theatre.

In 1600 the boys' companies regained their licenses. This put renewed pressure on the professional adults.

> Having tamed their audience, the common players now found themselves exposed to a new threat by these puny competitors, whose chief asset and weapon was a saucy frankness.[213]

After the reopening, the Chapel Royal resumed production of many of their previously popular plays. These were poorly received, however, because they proved to be sadly out of date. Slowly the theatre introduced the works of younger playwrights. A form of "new tragedy" gained great box office appeal. These were usually gory works based upon the Seneca model. The children engaged in various depictions of murder, mutilation and incest. These were performed very seriously with little humor and satire. Both Martson and Dekker

---

[212]Reese, *Shakespeare and His World and Work*, pp. 69-70.
[213]Bradbrook, *The Rise of the Common Player*, p. 213.

contributed to this genre and made considerable money from staging these violent classical epics.[214] Satiric comedies were still included in their repertory, but they became increasingly vicious and bawdy.

After 1600 the history of the boys' companies includes numerous examples of conflict and government censorship. Marston and Jonson continued a personal quarrel and used the child actors as mouthpieces for their slander.[215] In 1604 the children of the Chapel Royal, then called the children of the Queen's Revels appeared before the council on charges that a recent play had abused the name of the Earl of Essex. The managers were severely reprimanded for this infraction. In 1605 Chapman, Jonson and Marston co-authored a comedy entitled *Eastward Ho*. This stirred considerable controversy for a supposed "sardonic" reference to the Scots. Chapman and Jonson were arrested and imprisoned, while Marston fled the country.[216]

In 1606 the boys at Blackfriars produced John Day's *The Isle of Gulls*. The headmaster at that time, Henry Evans, defended himself before the magistrate. He was sentenced to a term in Bridewell prison, and it is possible that several of the children were also sent to that institution. He stated the reason for the closing of his theatre in a handbill, "...some of the boys being committed to prison by order of his Highness,..."[217] Late in 1608 the French Ambassador complained that a play at Blackfriars showed the French queen in a bad way. He said further that the play included a depiction of King James as "a drunk, violent and blaspheming character."[218] The theatre was forced to change management, but the new directors continued to produce their annual Christmas show before the King.

---

[214]Chute, *Shakespeare of London*, p. 230.

[215]Halliday, *Shakespeare and His Age*, p. 237.

[216]Chapman and Jonson were held for an extended time with the theatre threat of having their noses cut off. According to them, Martson was the real culprit. Ibid., p. 238.

[217]Chute, *Shakespeare of London*, p. 289.

[218]Leech, *The Revels History of Drama in English*, p. 111.

The eventual result of these accusations was increasing government censorship of the company at Blackfriars and other professional children's troupes. These restrictions removed the social satire and bawdry from the boys' productions. Once the shocking parody was gone, the audience quickly lost interest in the novelty of the child actors. Finally the company was limited to a short list of safe plays. New works were submitted to very strict censorship by the Master of Revels.[219] The treatment of the boys themselves also changed in the later years of professional production:

> When the children were revived, they became a species of common player put on by a group of citizens, actors and playwrights who had no interest in their education or their future.[220]

As Blackfriars became more of a professional producing organization and less an educational system, enrollment of upper class children began to drop. This presented the managers with numerous recruitment problems. The children's theatre needed a constant supply of young actors in order to maintain production levels. This forced the choirmasters to recruit new talent to fill the vacant positions left by the older boys. Often the managers were overly zealous in procuring new actors. As early as 1597 Nathaniel Giles was cited for abducting clever children from London schools and compelling them to act "by using the rod."[221] The citation did not have an effect upon the enlistment practices of Headmaster Giles, because in 1600 he was accused of kidnapping the son of a local gentleman. The father of Thomas Cliften brought the case to court. The deposition, signed by Henry Cliften, claimed that the lad was stolen off the streets to "exercyse the base trade of a mercynary enterlude player, to his utter lose of tyme, ruyne and disparagment...amongst a companie of lewde and dissolute players."[222] When the father approached Giles and demanded that his son be

---

[219]Harrison, *Elizabethan Plays and Players*, p. 40.

[220]Bradbrook, *The Rise of the Common Player*, p. 213.

[221]Schelling, *Elizabethan Drama*, p. 116.

[222]Harrison, *Elizabethan Plays and Players*, p.236.

returned, he was bluntly refused. Thomas was given a script and told to memorize the part or he would be beaten. Master Cliften went to his friend on the council, Sir John Fortescu, and within twenty-four hours the boy was released. This case was highly publicized and did nothing to improve the declining reputation of the Blackfriars theatre.

In 1606 the problem had reached such proportions that King James issued a mandate against forceful recruitment of choirboys.

> Provided always and we do straightly charge and command that none of the said Choristers or Children of the Chapel so to be taken by force of this commission shall be used or employed as Comedians or Stage players or to exercise or act any stage plays, interludes, Comedies, or tragedies for that it is not meet or decent that such as should sing the praises of God Almighty should be trained up or employed in such lascivious and profane exercises.[223]

Some critics have maintained that in spite of the sensational incidents the position of choirboy was an enviable education, even in the last years of the company's existence.

> ...we learn that the royal chapels were not always filled by legalized kidnappings, and that in any case the posts were held to be desirable.[224]

Whatever the causes for the closing of the children's companies, I believe it is clear that the pressure of professional production forced the managers to spend less time on the education of the boys. This shift in focus contributed to their decline, but the major reason for their final failure was that the fashion had changed.

> For a time these impudent topicalities and personal exchanges had an immense vogue: on the lips of the talented children they were pert, daring and, for a limited circle, amusing. So long as they wore the gloss of novelty, they won spectators from the professional companies and caused the professionals much anxiety. But as the novelty wore off, and their dramatists thought more about topicality than about the fundamental

---

[223]Shapiro, *Children of Revels*, p. 27.
[224]Newcombe, *The Child Actors*, p. 199.

principles of playmaking, they began to strain too hard after sensation and inevitably fell into indiscretions which brought them trouble.[225]

Ironically, the Children of St. Paul's never experienced the censorship that plagued the boys of the Chapel Royal.

> While satiric comedy was their forte, the St. Paul's Boys seem to have avoided the sort of direct contemporary references that embroiled the other children's company in frequent controversy; and they appear to have been wound up, quietly enough in 1607 -- why we do not know.[226]

The end of these companies may have been associated with the withdrawal of official patronage. Well before Elizabeth I died in 1603, her interest in the young players had diminished.

> It may be no coincidence that the Queen's delight in child players fell off at a time when she might be supposed past the age to hope for children of her own.[227]

Her successor devised his own courtly entertainment. He preferred the magnificent masques and seemed to have little taste for the boys' satiric word-play.

> The boy companies were less popular at the court under James than they had been under Elizabeth, as the most fashionable form of court entertainment under the new sovereign became the court masque, which Jonson and Jones elaborated into dazzling spectacle.[228]

The boys' satire was known to be directed at the King himself. Every aspect of his life was subject to the boys' slander. As his reign progressed, he found them less humorous and more irritating.

> Because the plays acted there (Blackfriars) frequently satirized James, his new Scots knights, his love of hunting, and his silver mines, the King apparently no longer wished to supply the troupe with choristers from his own chapel.[229]

---

[225]Reese, *Shakespeare and His World and Work*, p. 225.

[226]Leech, *The Revels History of Drama in English*, pp. 110-111.

[227]Bradbrook, *The Rise of the Common Player*, p. 215.

[228]Shapiro, *Children of Revels*, p. 29.

[229]Ibid., p. 27.

Although the boys' company became more professional, it lost its identity as an amateur producing organization and replacing its original educational intent with monetary goals, their manner of stage presentation affected the style of English theatre in the years to come.

> Indeed, in later years this company may have looked more and more like a normal adult troupe, and eventually the boys themselves, like the best of their plays, were absorbed into the regular public theatre. By the same token their practice of indoor performances in a small house by artificial lighting did not die with them, but was continued, as we have seen by Burbage and the King's Men. The heyday of boys' companies in the seventeenth century was brief, but their influence was lasting.[230]

Certainly, the drama of the Jacobean period was deeply influenced by the violence and bawdry of the young players.

> It has been said that the children's companies initiated the tragedy of sex and violence in the Jacobean period. The more impersonal the actor, the more dissociated he is in the audiences mind from what he projects as a professional, at he greater the freedom of the dramatist to explore and take risks.[231]

When theatre returned after the Commonwealth, popular comedy closely resembled the satiric works mounted first by the children's companies.

When producing popular drama, the managers were forced by necessity to ignore the boys' education. Although this shift in emphasis paid lucratively in the short run, slowly the pool of talent began to dry up. Since the children's companies lacked the self-perpetuating apprentice system of the adult theatres, they were forced constantly to recruit lesser talents. While the adult companies may have needed only three or four boys, the choirs needed many times that number in order to produce. The boy actors in the adult troupe could eventually become shareholders if they were persistent enough. This dream encouraged a dedication among the youngsters and contributed to a general ensemble feeling. No such goal existed for the boys company members. When their voices changed,

---

[230]Leech, *The Revels History of Drama in English*, p. 112.

[231]Dusinberre, *Shakespeare and the Nature of Women*, p. 270.

they were turned out with little hope of finding an outlet for their skills. Unable to break into the strict apprentice system of the adult companies, the boys were left to search out other trades in unrelated areas.

CHAPTER IV

THE BARD IN CLASS:

CONTEMPORARY APPROACHES TO TEACHING SHAKESPEARE

Miranda: Oh brave new world that has such people in't.
Prospero: 'Tis new to thee![232]

Each succeeding generation seems to rediscover the poetry and power of Shakespeare's writings. Since most peoples' initial exposure to the Bard comes through the vehicle of the high school English class, it is vital to examine present teaching methods before making any recommendations. The old aphorism "Shakespeare is the most taught and least read of all the poets,"[233] seems to point an accusing finger at the modern English teacher. Certainly many students view Shakespeare works as merely an exercise in academics -- bitter medicines which must be swallowed but never tasted. My experience as a teacher indicates that of those students who have read the Bard in high school, many express some animosity even toward his name. Others utter adulation but confess a sense of confusion in the presence of such awesome works. One is left to make one of two conclusions: 1) Shakespeare's plays are not within the intellectual reach of the average student. 2) Current teaching methods have not stimulated students to appreciate the material.

It is hard to accept the first conclusion when we assess Shakespeare's world-wide popularity. France and Germany have produced his plays for

---

[232]*The Tempest*, act 3, sc. 2, lines 183-184.
[233]Robert B. Heilman, Shakespeare in the Classroom: Object vs. Immediate Experience," in *Teaching Shakespeare*, ed. Walter Edens, Christopher Durer, Walter Eggers, Duncan Harris, Keith Hull, (Princeton, N.J.: Princeton University Press, 1977), p. 3.

centuries, and today he is one of the most popular playwrights in Japan. Recent visitors to Siberia report frequent and popular revivals of his works.

> Shakespeare, on the screen, on the stage, or in print, apparently receives the approval of Soviet dialectians, who do not require him to masquerade as a party spokesman, though a recent Moscow radio program announced that Shakespeare's works have a "certain affinity to Socialist realism" and that Soviet writers shared a "kinship" with him. On both sides of the Iron Curtain Shakespeare has admirers, and he is one writer who is apparently above and beyond the turmoil of international politics.[234]

Thus one can not argue with Shakespeare's popularity and apparent universality. After all, Shakespeare was a writer by profession, and his survival depended upon his practical ability to reach the masses:

> In approaching Shakespeare, we must remember that he wrote, not for a small group of intellectuals, but for everyman, from coutier to apprentice, for the man in the street, for anyone who could be lured to pay a penny or a tuppence to get into the theatre to see a play. Shakespeare wrote with one or both eyes on the box office. He wanted to be popular and he tried to write in such a manner and on such themes that everyman would welcome his efforts -- and pay for them.[235]

Shakespeare became very popular during his time, but inspite of this success, he remained an experimental and creative writer. It would have been quite easy for him to repeat a proven formula after the rewards of a money-making script. His craft continued vital and experimental. He seemed conscious of the Renaissance notion of "invention" and exercised his imagination by drawing from a multitude of sources. Variations in form and content evidenced a genius for experimentation, and this continued throughout his professional career.

> One characteristic that emerges most strongly about Shakespeare is his experimental turn of mind. Once he began a project, he continued it with enthusiasm and a sense of commitment, but when the play was

---

[234]Louis B. Wright, "Shakespeare for Everyman," in *Shakespeare in School and College*, ed. National Council of Teachers of English, (Champaign, IL.: National Council of Teachers of English, 1964), p. 5.

[235]Ibid., p.8.

finished, he never returned to that same sort of play again, no matter how successful. In Renaissance terms, he shows remarkable "invention," which is the ability to find something to say in its appropriate form -- what we would call imaginative fecundity -- or creative genius. Shakespeare is constantly trying out different kinds of plays -- beginning at the beginning again, as it were -- when he could have comfortably remained in his own area of competence. He makes a special point of not repeating himself, and even his failures or partial failures are interesting and vital, and his work as a whole shows a notable capacity for growth. Like Picasso, Shakespeare flourishes in an astonishing variety of styles and media. He seems to be as much concerned with pleasing himself as his audience, and he offers an excellent example of what it means to be lively in the arts.[236]

Although high school students often are exposed to only a limited selection of William Shakespeare's most famous plays, recently teachers have been assigning a wider variety and including comedies on the required reading lists. This trend includes comedies with the list of famous tragedies. In this way students get a more varied sampling of the range of his artistic genius.

Shakespeare is again becoming a "must" in United States high schools. Eighth graders, if carefully directed in their study, often read with delight *A Midsummer Night's Dream*. Recently the custom in high schools is to read one Shakespearean play a year, if that much, but the trend is not to include several of Shakespeare's dramas each year.

With no special theme for the freshman anthologies, the inclusion of one of the excellent paperback editions is easy. And increasingly the succeeding years can be enriched by one of the "Bard's" plays. Some schools have required the students to read 12 Shakespearean plays during their four years in high school.

A survey of 22 high schools in Washington and Colorado showed the following being taught successfully to high school students: *Comedy of Errors, Taming of the Shrew, Midsummer Night's Dream, Henry IV, parts I and II, Henry V, Romeo and Juliet, Merchant of Venice, As You Like It, Julius Caesar, Hamlet, Othello, King Lear, Macbeth*, and *Twelfth Night*.[237]

---

[236]Maurice Charney, *How to Read Shakespeare*, (New York: McGraw-Hill, 1971), p. 145.

[237]Florence M. Diesman, "Shakespeare in High School Today," *Journal of Secondary Education* 40 (March 1965), p. 131.

With this great variety of the Bard's plays it is amazing that there still seems to be a general dislike and misunderstanding about the nature of Shakespeare's writings. Students often complain that he bores them, and this feeling can be carried throughout adulthood. Recently I met a sixty year old man who was responsible for distributing grant monies from several large foundations. He confessed that he disliked Shakespeare. He blamed this animosity on a high school English teacher. Since that experience, more than forty years earlier, he had neither read nor seen a Shakespearean play.

> Since Shakespeare's value is and has been appreciated for many generations, it is probably correct to say that most failures in awakening student enthusiasm are attributable to a lack of "knowledge" of the subject and a lack of method to apply what is known.

> When we find that many teachers write articles complaining that their students are bored, that they find Shakespeare too ancient, that "Shakespeare is a name which serves merely to produce shivers," or that they "hate" Shakespeare, the college professor may well wonder what he has taught his future teachers which has sent them out to leave such impressions in the minds of their students.[238]

Because of this prevalent attitude, many educators are insisting that methods of teaching be adapted to the needs of the students.

> Shakespeare, throughout the world, is both the most studied literary subject and the common factor in many people's acquaintance with literary culture. But during the past ten or twenty years there have been protests against the academic way with Shakespeare. Teachers, students, scholars and critics have all been arranged for limiting the effectiveness of Shakespeare's plays by their own attempts to understand and explain.[239]

Although a standardized method may not be possible, it is necessary to evaluate present methods in terms of their effectiveness.

> If we are to use Shakespeare as a means of enriching minds, refining tastes, exercising intellects, stimulating imaginations, deepening

---

[238]Louis Marder, "Teaching Shakespeare: Is There a Method?". *College English* 40 (April 1964): 481.

[239]John Russell Brown, *Free Shakespeare*, (London: Heineman Press, 1974), p. 96.

sympathies, developing emotional maturity, and stimulating love for literature -- worthy goals to say the least -- we must think not of merely teaching Shakespeare but think of doing it the best way possible.[240]

Successful teaching is dependent upon many variables. The search for the ultimate teaching method may prove futile, but there can be no argument that present methods desperately need improvement. A recent survey indicated that nearly half the participants had negative feelings toward Shakespeare -- attitudes which had been imparted largely by their high school English teachers.[241]

Discussions abound concerning the proper age to introduce students to these plays. Some teachers have reported success at even a very early age.

First graders see nothing formidable about Shakespeare's plays. They don't, that is, if you introduce Shakespeare to them in child-size pieces -- selected for child-size interests. The children may not always understand the message of the literature. But they do envision their own versions of the scenes described and they do enjoy the rhythmic power of the words.

A very important ingredient in introducing Shakespeare to first graders is the teacher's own love for his works. I could not have roused interest and enthusiasm among my first-graders had I not so loved Shakespeare myself that I wanted to share him with them and was determined to find a way to do it.[242]

The "child-size pieces" recommended by the above writer include the witches from *Macbeth* and the fairy dance from *A Midsummer Night's Dream*. Although these short selections did not really acquaint first graders with Shakespeare, they did encourage enjoyment and participation. When later asked by visiting parents who was their favorite writer, they invariably answered "Shakespeare." It is to be hoped that they carried this experience through high school.

---

[240]Marder, "Teaching Shakespeare," p. 487.

[241]Survey taken by the author, Thursday, July 29, 1982. The symposium discussion followed a production of *Romeo and Juliet* by the Indianapolis Shakespeare Festival. This project was funded by the Indiana Committee for the Humanities and was titled "Shakespeare Without Tears: Education Outside the Classroom." It is interesting to note that of the balance of my respondents, very few were indifferent to Shakespeare. Many loved Shakespeare and traced their interest to one excellent teacher who read his words well.

[242]Barbara Heeden, "Shakespeare in First Grade," *Grade Teacher* 82 (October 1964): 91.

Most students are introduced to the Bard later in their education. The question often arises about whether ninth graders have the knowledge of language and literature necessary to interpret the words of our greatest playwright.

> When the day came on which I had planned to have my ninth-graders begin to study Shakespeare, I was apprehensive. The year before I had read *Lear* with a class of tenth-graders and, although most of them had been sensitive to the human dilemmas expressed in the play, many of them had trouble with the language. Would Shakespeare seem like a foreign tongue to ninth graders? I had thought long about it and still was not sure just what I would do in class. I had no doubts that Shakespeare had many things to offer all human beings, and the knowledge and enjoyment of his work was a goal I wanted for these students. Some of them would be reading him for the first time, and I wanted to help them make a good beginning on a lifelong project of learning to enjoy and find meaning in Shakespeare. It seemed to me that for ninth graders it was breaking through the barrier of the language that had to be the first step. They had to be able to read the play before they could react to it with ideas and emotions.[243]

This understanding of content is crucial before a student can undertake an evaluation of theme, characterization or poetry, but with the limited exposure to literature most students have received through elementary school and junior high school, few are prepared for classical masterpieces early in high school. Perhaps the solution is to postpone the introduction of Shakespeare until later.

> It is difficult to determine on what level to begin the teaching of Shakespeare. From my own experience in the junior high schools, I would judge that the full meaning of Shakespeare's ideas, the appreciation of his literary talents, and the enjoyment of his poetic style can be best transmitted to *not less than* an average ninth year class or a bright eighth grade class. Suffice it to say that an individual teacher must determine the level based on his own experience.[244]

Some even feel that ninth grade is too early.

---

[243]Martha Treichler, "Free Acting Shakespeare." *The Independent School Bulletin* 31 (May 1972): 64.

[244]Bernard Hanwerker, When Should Shakespeare be Taught in the Schools," *High Points* (March 1961): 69.

While some gifted eighth graders may be ready for Shakespearean comedy, the likelihood is that Shakespeare is best introduced to better groups in grade nine, and regular students in grade ten.[245]

Postponing the introduction of Shakespeare until the age of sixteen seems a serious error. Having witnessed thousands of children sit with rapt attention during two hours of Shakespeare, it is my belief that love for Shakespeare can be kindled among the young. Why is it that these same children who are so fascinated by the Bard in performance find him so difficult to understand when merely read? Academics tend to think of Shakespeare as something which must be comprehended and not merely enjoyed. Children who are spell-bound by the magic of the fairies and the impishness of Puck in A *Midsummer Night's Dream* are not judging "the full meaning of Shakespeare's ideas." When the only goal of a teacher is complete comprehension on the part of the students, the entrancement of Shakespeare's theatrics will be lost. As a director of Shakespeare, I am continually confronted with English teachers with their own personal views on Shakespearean production. Many harbor a belief that Shakespeare should be uncut and unchanged. If a production is enjoyable, teachers tend to suspect that the poetry has been lost. This may seem like a condemnation of educators by a bitter theatrical artist, but it is no way intended to be a blanket generalization. Teachers seem to be infected on an international level with "Bardolotry" to use George Bernard Shaw's phrase. We have made a divine creation of this writer, and our presentation tends to alienate him from our students. Shaw was one of the first writers to recognize this idol worship and question its effect:

> We are disposed to agree that we are making too much of a fetish of our Swan. He was the greatest intellect we have produced, but the tendency to regard him as above criticism is bad. Shakespeare is supreme

---

[245]Glayds Veidemanis, "Shakespeare in the High School Classroom," Wright, *Shakespeare in School and College*, p. 61.

because he embodied most completely the whole range of emotions, and his greatness is due to that fact.[246]

We must present Shakespeare in human terms and remember that he wrote interesting popular theatre. Shaw spent much of his early life disliking Shakespeare for a variety of reasons. Most of these opinions were formed when he was still a student. Later in his life he realized the humanity in these great works. "When I began to write, William was a divinity and a bore. Now he is a fellow-creature."[247] It is this fellow-creature that will invariably excite our reticent students. We must allow his personal dramas to speak for themselves. D. Allen Carroll discussed the tendency of teachers to over-adulate Shakespeare and concluded that we must let the Bard do his own talking. He addressed the teachers:

> ...when we read Shakespeare, as we shall, in great swatches in every session, we shall read him well. Read with a sensitivity to tone and with confidence which comes from practice, he has the power to renew our spirits and move our students. We can trust him.[248]

Before discussing the various methods used to acquaint students with these plays, it is necessary to recognize the difficulty of the task. Research into teaching methods can often be misleading as Veidemanis points out:

> The testimony of English teachers in various, educational journals, conveys quite a different impression. The typical article is a glowing success story, presenting, for example, enthusiastic accounts of eighth graders or sophomores who have adeptly avoided the major reading pitfalls, gone off independently on their own into *Lear* or *Othello*, and produced penetrating discussions on Shakespeare's psychological insights and contemporary outlook. Most of these articles also manage to imply (rather explicitly!) that the writer has found a sure-fire way of avoiding all teaching mistakes that once made the study of Shakespeare for him such a tedious bore when he was a student in some unenlightened English class. After reading of such achievements, we may, like Brutus, feel compelled to abandon our stars and suffer indictment for personal

---

[246]Edwin Wilson, *Shaw on Shakespeare*, New York: Dodd, Mead and Company, 1961), p. xiv.
[247]Ibid.
[248]D. Allen Carroll, "The Presentation of Shakespeare, " in Wright, *Shakespeare in School an d College*, p. 62.

inadequacies and unimaginative teaching. These blithe success stories, however, frankly leave me skeptical. In all honestly, it is impossible to avoid the recognition that both the teaching and the studying of Shakespeare are exacting, often frustrating tasks, necessitating thorough, perceptive, informed study, for which there are no painless shortcuts or easy formulas. Lasting appreciation can never be won by merely trying to "unbury the bard" or "get a kick out of Will."[249]

Ideally, teaching must assume a variety of different goals. When approaching Shakespeare we must find a method which confronts his literature in a number of different ways. We should not expect any single method to meet educational goals adequately, but certainly several should be enumerated. Louis Marder lists four classifications.

> With no intention of being exhaustive we may readily admit the following goals as among those the well informed teacher is seeking to achieve in an interesting and stimulating manner:

> *Literary*: appreciation and enjoyment of drama as a genre with its subdivisions of farce, comedy, tragedy, history, and romance; Shakespeare's Language, poetry and structure.

> *Dramatic*: history of the theatre, stage, acting, dramatic reading and interpretation.

> *Social*: understanding of mankind and his culture through moral, religious, ethical, political, philosophical, historical, economic and social aspects of drama.

> *Personal*: self-development, imaginative exercise, ability to understand man under tension, the ability to laugh at life, the ability to listen, read, observe, think, speak, and write.[250]

Though the preceding goals might readily be accepted by almost all teachers, in practice the possibilities for student growth seem limited. Many critics have accused the school teachers of falling far short of these educational ideals:

> The charge is sometimes made that Shakespeare is kept alive by a conspiracy of school teachers. I wish that this were true, for it would

---

[249]Veidemanis, "Shakespeare in the High School Classroom," p. 55.
[250]Marder, "Teaching Shakespeare," p. 480.

prove that teachers are more effective than they are. On the contrary, I am certain that Shakespeare has survived in spite of what school teachers have done to him...So much for the teachers' conspiracy. Shakespeare does not stay alive because of academicians. Devoted scholars, it is true, lavish millions of man-hours trying to explain him, but their efforts touch only peripherally the average non-academic reader of the plays.[251]

The typical English teacher has been instructed through years of graduate seminars to treat the Shakespearean play as an academic puzzle which requires a certain enlightened rationale to put together. Or as Robert B. Heilman writes, "The Shakespeare canon became a kind of anatomical specimen for dissection..."[252] And as the vivisectionist of the goose that laid the golden eggs found, once the poor bird had been separated into its various components, its life and subsequent treasures were gone.

This brings us to examine the traditional techniques of teaching Shakespeare. Although this method has received much recent criticism it is still avidly practiced by most English teachers. Laurence McNamee criticizes this manner of teaching:

> In the traditional approach the teacher will assign the first act "to be read for tomorrow." This assignment may include the mandate to look up all obsolete words, an excellent device for proving to the student that Shakespeare is dull! When class convenes, our teacher will have certain students read certain roles aloud, which is alright when it works, only it doesn't work. It doesn't work because of the aesthetic principle that the next step from the sublime is the ridiculous, and Shakespeare's magnificent poetry can too easily be brought down from ethereal sublimity to the nadir of grotesque.[253]

Often for this reason, teachers do not let the students read Shakespeare aloud in the classroom. Their method then becomes one of discussing the previous night's readings which the students may or may not have understood. Although these class discussions may clarify plot, they may miss other elements of his plays.

---

[251]Wright, *Shakespeare for Everyman*, pp. 7-8.

[252]Robert B. Heilman, "Shakespeare in the Classroom," in *Teaching Shakespeare*, p. 7.

[253]Laurence McNamee, "New Horizons in the Teaching of Shakespeare," *College English*, 23 (April 1962): 584.

Often students report that they gain very little from reading the Bard's work silently. Discussions have some effect in channeling comprehension:

> (A high school) in Spokane, Washington, which employs team teaching, used the Adler method, giving each student a list of questions to answer as he reads the play silently. Upon the next meeting of the class, in seminar groups of twelve to seventeen members, all are sure they have not learned much from the play, but thirty minutes of discussion helps them realize how much they have derived on their own, as do later seminars.[254]

The study questions seem to improve the effectiveness of the traditional home study method. The questions focus the students' attention on specific sections of the text, but they may not contribute to overall comprehension. The teacher is unable to control that silent reading done by the student in the home. "All of us know that the true course in Shakespeare takes place not so much in our presence as outside, whenever and wherever our students read Shakespeare."[255] I question if Shakespeare can be interpreted adequately when read in front of the television set with a myriad of surrounding distractions. Young students may find their first reading exceedingly difficult. "When we are reading plays for the first time, especially if we are unused to reading plays, we find it difficult to be fully aware of their dynamic movement."[256] We seem to expect a great deal from our students. Traditional education does not demand the kind of active participation which Shakespearean study demands.

> By and large they (the students) expect the teacher's role will be active, theirs passive, and they grow impatient with extensive participation by any of the other thirty-five or so members of the class.[257]

Many have complained that these discussion periods often lack organization and are counterproductive to the student's study of the play itself.

---

[254]Diesman, "Shakespeare in High School Today," p. 133.

[255]Carroll, "The Presentation of Shakespeare," p. 54.

[256]Bernard Beckerman, "Shakespeare's Plays as Works of Drama," in *Teaching Shakespeare*, p. 312.

[257]Carroll, "The Presentation of Shakespeare," p. 50.

Hence classroom bull sessions, predominantly casual and directionless, and often mistaken for exercises in group therapy. Thus we take out our hang-ups rather than take in what might help make things hang together (or hold seances in which student mediums make the dead Shakespeare behave and speak just like those who call him up).[258]

In the traditional method these classroom discussions are often supplemented by lectures by the teachers on theatrical practices during Shakespeare's time.

Because the plays were intended to be acted and on a particular stage, we teach a good deal about the construction of the Elizabethan stage and about its conventions and we otherwise try to develop a consciousness in our students of the requirements of theatre.[259]

Although the intentions of this historical approach are excellent, in practice the students attention may be shifted away from the plays themselves. Robert Speaight warns teachers of this pitfall:

Knowledge of the layout of the Globe Theatre, the facts of Shakespeare's life, or the clothing, customs, and history of Elizabeth I's reign can indisputably enrich a student's background; yet, these considerations, over-emphasized, can also become substitute for and barriers to genuine reading and analysis of the play.[260]

Maurice Charney agrees that stressing the historical aspects of Shakespeare's theatre may be avoiding student confrontation with the script:

I have been assuming throughout this book that Shakespeare is accessible to intelligent readers and spectators without any special training. We must remember that Shakespeare wrote his plays for a popular audience. Although they have a complexity of design and expression that repays careful study, the plays are not learned in any true sense of the word. I don't agree with the common feeling that only by knowing a great deal about Shakespeare's background can we possibly qualify as readers of his works. It is exhilarating to put oneself into the Elizabethan World picture, or even into the more homely aspects of Elizabethan life and thought. But social and intellectual history is not the same thing as

---

[258]Heilman, "Shakespeare in the Classroom," p. 12.

[259]Carroll, "The Presentation of Shakespeare," p. 60.

[260]Veidemanis, "Shakespeare in the High School Classroom," p. 55.

literature, and the background should never become a barrier to the direct experience of the works.[261]

Although the traditional method of assigned readings and subsequent discussions seems to prevail in American schools, there are many indications that this system may not be serving the needs of the students.

> Few university teachers are satisfied with their system, yet few are willing to do anything to change it. We teachers are in danger of becoming a class adept at criticism, yet either unable or unwilling to carry out the consequences of our criticism into action and reform.[262]

Perhaps many teachers are not conscious of the alternatives to the traditional methods. Students are not used to actively participating in their own education. There seems to be an acute sense of frustration on the part of many teachers. They complain that they are trapped an ineffective system which seems to discourage enjoyment of the works of Shakespeare.

> I have used whatever ways and critical approaches were needed to remedy ignorance, stock expectations, faulty response, failure to respond, or whatever seemed to stand between students and a full, informed, sensitive, and personal response to Shakespeare's plays. I was never satisfied with what I had accomplished. I found the students failed -- because I failed them -- to understand the plays sufficiently to be able to process them. They understood separate scenes but not the whole play, and their knowledge of separate plays was not cumulative and progressive. Later I realized that meaning is a function of context: the meaning of any part of a play is given by its context in the play,...[263]

The apparently simple revelation to the above writer points up why students can appreciate Shakespeare on the stage and not in the textbook. The theatrical production tends to be viewed as a unified event. It is thematically self-contained. Actions give meaning to the written words and characterization brings life to the script. These writings must retain their dramatic elements in the classroom or they will be dissected for symbolism as if they were merely long poems.

---

[261]Charney, "How to Read Shakespeare," p. 144.

[262]Brian Vickers, "Teaching Coriolanus: The Importance of Perspective," in *Teaching Shakespeare*, p. 229.

[263]A.C. Hamilton, "The Case of Measure for Measure," in *Teaching Shakespeare*, p. 96.

... if we continue to teach plays as if they were long poems, no matter how many times we punctuate our close readings with assertions that we are not really forgetting that plays are plays, students will continue to learn about a piece of a play instead of the whole thing.[264]

If we have indeed failed our students, we must thoroughly analyze the failures of the present teaching programs. Seven criticisms were enumerated by Gladys Veidemanis:

1) Too much time spent on unrelated art and history projects; too little concentrated attention on the written text itself.

2) Over-exhaustive study of a single play -- bleeding it dry. (Would we not do better to adhere to the maxim: "Better to underteach than to over teach"?)

3) Too much attention to footnotes, criticism, emendations to the extent that the play becomes burdened beyond the difficulties it already presents of itself.

4) Too much "rapture" or virtuousness surrounding the venture -- the feeling that "at last we are on something really worthwhile, and even though this is painful, it's good for you!"

5) Too much teacher reading and explication with too little endeavor to teach students to read and comprehend Shakespeare for themselves.

6) Too much popularizing or trying overhard to make Shakespeare "hip" or "a snap"; using comic books or cheapened versions which eliminate the flavor of the original style.

7) Pushing Shakespeare on students who are too immature to handle it or are incapable.[265]

Most educators who have attempted the study of the Bard in class have probably made some of these mistakes. Our desire to make Shakespeare palatable often renders him indigestible to the students. Teachers must realize the limitations of the classroom itself:

---

[264]Morris Eaves, "The Real Thing: A Plan for Producing Shakespeare in the Classroom," *College English* 31 (February 1970): p. 463.

[265]Veidemanis, "Shakespeare in the High School Classroom," p. 56.

> The classroom imposes certain limitations on a teacher's method -
> - for instance, he cannot just deliver an interpretation and walk away, as
> the critic does who publishes an essay or book on Shakespeare. The
> teacher's audience is ever present, and articulate.[266]

The teacher's goal must remain student focused. The love of the beauty and skill

of Shakespeare's writing will be eternally planted if the instructor lets the plays

speak for themselves. Students will carry a love of Shakespeare long after the

specific details of an historical study have been forgotten.

> The difficult task for any teacher, of course, is to let students see
> Shakespeare's "sparkling chips," showing not how they flatten into empty
> generalizations but how they form an integrated dramatic statement, how
> the disparate parts of a Shakespeare play grow "to something of great
> constancy."[267]

The teacher must personalize his teaching methods. He must love the Bard and

share that excitement with his class. Perhaps this kind of teaching requires a

special teacher.

> The teacher is not Shakespeare -- he presents Shakespeare. For the
> most part, his tasks are to use words which, while not poetry, are poetic
> in kind, that is, words which excite the imagination, and to give his
> remarks a form which, while not drama, is dramatic, that is, a form
> which activates, intensifies, and resolves expectations through exploration
> and discovery. Ideally the classroom lecture is an art form, with special
> conventions, although, like the sermon, it is a minor one.[268]

This seems to be expecting too much from the ordinary teacher. It is

difficult to imagine all educators treating every classroom lecture as an art form.

The demand that they try to adopt poetic diction for instructing Shakespeare

seems impractical. But the above quotation does emphasize the need for a

modified approach when dealing with dramatic art in the classroom. Many critics

are calling for research in this area.

---

[266]Vickers, "Teaching Coriolanus," p. 228.

[267]Albert Werthern, "The Reteaching and Regreening of Macbeth," in *Teaching Shakespeare*, p. 115.

[268]Carroll, "The Presentation of Shakespeare," pp. 48-49.

Somehow, the way must be found to an approach that is mature, yet not stuffy; scholarly, without being pedantic; dramatic, yet also literary; thorough, but not exhausting; contemporary as well as universal.[269]

The most popular way to vary the "home study method" is for the teacher to read the plays to the students in class. Since most English teachers are inexperienced in oral interpretation their reading skills may limit the student's comprehension.

A second solution is for the teacher to do all the reading, but this puts too much pressure on the teacher, who has the additional problem of maintaining discipline, and also puts too much pressure on the poor student who would have to listen to the same voice for fifty odd minutes.[270]

Having had experience with a college teacher who read Shakespeare to his students in an unrelenting Southern drawl, I can attest to the monotony of this method. Even a skilled reader can deprive students of the essential Shakespeare.

It is also not uncommon for the Shakespearean unit to become the vehicle for a teacher's extended virtuoso performance, surely highly relaxing for the students, since they are left almost nothing to do but sit back and admire, but hardly educating.[271]

Many might disagree that hearing Shakespeare read is not truly educating our students. On the other hand an actress working with the Indianapolis Shakespeare Festival confessed that both her love of acting and the Bard were generated by the "inspired" readings of a high school teacher. Many others confess a similar source for their appreciation of Shakespeare's plays.

The simple truth is that Shakespeare's verbal magic works principally upon the ear. The printed page, the picture, the stage setting meant nothing to the Bard. He expected the imagination to do one-half of the playing (as he tells us in the prologue of *Henry V*), and the organ he attacks is the ear. I concede that millions of devotees have been won to Shakespeare via the printed page, but I firmly believe that most of them were won because "professor so-and-so could really read Shakespeare."

---

[269]Veidemanis, "Shakespeare in the High School Classroom," p. 56.

[270]McNamee, "New Horizons in the Teaching of Shakespeare," p. 584.

[271]Veidemanis, "Shakespeare in the High School Classroom," pp. 55-56.

I further concede that in the past the classroom instruction was necessarily dependent on the printed page.[272]

Many of these charmed students are captivated not by the action of the play or by the depth of characterization, but by the vocal abilities of their teacher.

> I allude to the classroom actor who triumphs through the master's voice: Less a taker of roles than a vocalist, to whom the usual tribute is "He reads so beautifully." What we get from him, in place of the dramatic object to be apprehended, is an aura of phonetic charm and acoustical seduction, an aural/oral (to borrow from science) hypnosis.[273]

I am not as willing to condemn these classroom actors. Any teacher with the power to capture the imagination and overcome the inherent bigotries of reticent students must be commended. If the students miss the complete experience of the text, they have most likely attained a positive attitude toward the Bard and the performance of his works, as in the case of the previously mentioned actress. She remembered the beauty of those high school sessions, and this remembrance encouraged more extensive study. Her love for Shakespeare is now based on a thorough knowledge of most of the initial plays, but she still credits her actor/teacher with stimulating her initial interest.

Other teachers report limited success with the oral reading technique. Martha Treichler avoided historical over-emphasis but found that she reached only part of her class.

> Since to me the play is the most important, I didn't want to get sidetracked into a biography of Shakespeare or into a discussion of the architecture of the Globe Theatre. But I did want them to know when Shakespeare had lived so that they would realize that the language they were reading was over three hundred and fifty years old. I asked them what they knew about Shakespeare, and together we pieced together the essential details. Then I began to read aloud from the play, throwing myself into the reading, overdoing it a little. Every speech or so I stopped and said, "Can you understand his language? What is he saying?" About half the class caught on fast,...[274]

---

[272]McNamee, "New Horizons in Teaching Shakespeare," p. 584.
[273]Heilman, "Shakespeare in the Classroom," p. 9.
[274]Treichler, "Free Acting Shakespeare," p. 64.

I would question the effectiveness of this method from the very beginning. The constant interruptions "every speech or so" could only disturb the continuity. This would be as disconcerting for the students as having to read the script cold while constantly referring to the footnotes to make sure they absorb every meaning. Though she felt slightly disappointed, it is surprising that the above teacher was as successful as she maintains. Capturing the imaginations of about half the class certainly attests to the success of any method of oral presentation.

A variant of this teacher-as-performer method is the approach of retelling the plot to the students. For several obvious reasons, this system achieves limited success.

> A third possibility is for the teacher to show slides of plot or to tell the story, perhaps in an Andy Griffith style. But here again (aside from the fact that "giving the plot" is not giving Shakespeare) we have a reversion to the overemphasis on the printed page.[275]

This system completely ignores the poetry in the plays. The teacher could supplement his narrative by inserting readings of selected speeches, but this demands a great deal from the teacher, who in most cases, lacks any dramatic training.

The increasing availability of recordings and electronic equipment would seem a solution to these presentation problems. Many instructors have reported successes when using recordings of great Shakespearean productions either on records or tapes. All of the Bard's plays can be bought or borrowed through libraries.

> With the great advances in tapes and records, we can give every student an aisle seat in the sixth row as he listens to the greatest actors in the English-speaking world.[276]

Recordings do not remove the necessity of script study. The play books are open in order for the students to follow the plot and read the poetry. Often records do not match published scripts. For production purposes, directors often

---

[275]McNamee, "New Horizons in Teaching Shakespeare," p. 584.
[276]Ibid.

change, edit or rearrange material. This adds another complication to the organization and preparation of the class.

> ...Provide the students with a text that follow, the recording line by line. Anything else is makeshift, haphazard, and destructive of the illusion. If such a text is not purchasable, then make one of your own and (after obtaining permission) mimeograph it. This is work, tedious work, but the rewards are exceedingly great.[277]

McNamee goes on to explain his method of utilizing recording as a supplement to class discussions.

> After passing out the sheets (*Macbeth*, for example), I limit my remarks to a few pertinent comments about the mood of the play...Then I quit explaining and let the poetry of Shakespeare do its own explaining. The best method is to play an entire act uninterruptedly during one class and go over the material the next class. If time is of the essence, one can insert short explanations by means of the convenient pause button now available on tape-recorders...Teachers will find that fewer explanations are needed than when one was tied to the printed text: obsolete words like "Zounds" become shockingly clear when fulminated by an excellent actor, and meaningless expletives like "indeed" take on a new light when intoned by a derisive Iago.[278]

Beckerman has utilized recordings in class and comments that they do not generate the same immediate effect as live performances.

> By contrast, teachers of music have at hand recordings of the best musicians. In addition, they themselves can usually illuminate a point by using the piano. Theoretically, teachers have the same resources. They too can play recordings or read a scene aloud. But Shakespeare recordings do not bear on the same proximity to the playwright that musical recordings bear on the actual performance of a score.[279]

Records do not have the accompanying action of live performances. The style of these recordings can present problems to the student. Often they are made from "classic" British productions which may be dry, lengthy and altogether alien to the American student. The temptation to interrupt the tape may clarify individual words and allusions, but this practice, as in reading footnotes, destroys dramatic

---

[277]Ibid., p. 285.
[278]Ibid.
[279]Beckerman, "Shakespeare's Plays as Works of Drama," pp. 313-314.

continuity. McNamee recommends playing the recording during a single class period. How often do teachers, at any level, have the luxury of an uninterrupted two or three hour slot? How many students would relish the idea of sitting in a classroom in which the only action is the periodic changing of records? There is the real danger that the class will minimize home study with the expectation that they will hear the play in class. Heilman discusses one wry good reason not to use recordings in the classroom.

> Although we can add English courses *ad infinitum*, we cannot add hours to the Shakespeare course, and every hour that goes for records and tapes is taken away from orderly discussion...Records, in brief, are entertainment and, like productions of the plays, belong in outside-class time.[280]

John Russell Brown suggests that the teacher find ways of letting students hear the texts outside of class.

> But simpler means are available. Shakespeare's imaginative range and fertility, and the free form of presentation for which he wrote, combine to make even a short passage from a play capable of awakening a recognition of the drama's endless life and suggestiveness. With a tape recorder a solitary student can begin to explore the text in sound.[281]

The mechanics of getting recording equipment to twenty or more students may be very complicated. Morris Eaves confesses that he is baffled by this problem.

> A set of phonograph records, perhaps the next best thing but a giant step beneath its betters, devours class time in a way that has not often seemed justifiable to me, and I have never been able to devise a satisfactory system for having students use records outside the classroom.[282]

At first impression, recordings would seem to solve many problems of the traditional methods. Recordings despite all their advantages, are still an auditory event and not a truly theatrical one. The most obvious solution is to show film

---

[280]Heilman, "Shakespeare in the Classroom," p. 11.

[281]Brown, *Free Shakespeare*, p. 106.

[282]Eaves, "The Real Thing," p. 463.

or videos of actual productions. Although these also occupy valuable class time, films give students a more accurate impression of production techniques.

Often teachers turn to film or video recording in order to supplement lectures and discussions about the film director's approach to the script. There is a tradition of using films in the classroom, and teachers have been extolling their virtues for years. "Of indispensable value, too, are the brilliant humanities films, especially those on *Oedipus* and *Hamlet*."[283] There are problems with this apparently easy method of bringing Shakespeare into the classroom. Many criticize the film media's limitations in presenting a work of literary art created for the stage. John Russell Brown argues that film severely hinders the student's appreciation of the theatrical art form.

> Some teachers have turned from the ardors of play production and substituted the provision of films, video-tapes and sound recordings so that the students can see and hear a wide range of alternative renderings of a scene or a whole play. They use these to start discussion among their students and indeed they do provide something like a serve-yourself theatre experience. But the experiment is without true audience contact with the play and without the physical reality of stage and performers, and it escapes from the excitement of real time. Moreover the camera has shown the audience where to look and how to look. The viewer is more passive, and his range of vision greatly limited. Even rapid experience of these wholly different productions of a single play seems to work against a true exploration of Shakespeare: they are seen so close together in time and are so wholly different in concept and filming procedures, that the large differences of presentation tend to leap to attention rather than the similarities or varieties implicit in a single intense moment. Attention is often drawn to acting and film techniques which are not subjects that can be appreciated or discussed responsibly without a great deal of specialized knowledge.[284]

Jay L. Halio shares these concerns. Film tends to popularize Shakespeare. He contends that these movies may entertain, but they do not educate their audiences.

> To some extent, this new availability of films and performances threatens to supplant the old reliance upon a close reading of the text

---

[283]Veidemanis, "Shakespeare in the High School Classroom," p. 61.
[284]Brown, *Free Shakespeare*, p. 105-106.

followed by lectures and discussions -- the usual format for undergraduate courses in Shakespeare. "Threaten" is, admittedly, a loaded word and reveals my own predilections, I suppose, although the main thrust of what I want to say here is to defend the use of Shakespeare in performance as a teaching technique. But there is no point in evading at the outset the concern that without proper care the study of Shakespeare could degenerate into entertainment without insight, a joyful but vacuous apprehension of the plays leading to, at best, a sophisticated appreciation of staging techniques or, at worst, a debased taste for gimmickry and horseplay. Alas, our modern theatre is not free of such degeneracy, its many superb accomplishments not withstanding.

What to do? I have two suggestions, neither of them especially original but each tested over a period of years with my own students with sufficient success to encourage me to recommend them to others. The first concerns the *critical* use of Shakespeare in performance. The other involves the students' own performance of scenes from Shakespeare.[285]

Since I will discuss the second suggestion in the following pages of this work, the first should be stressed. Since many English teachers lack experience in reviewing and criticizing theatrical productions, they resort to textual discussions and ignore staging and acting. Although Halio accuses theatre directors, I believe that films are more prone to tamper with the scripts of Shakespeare. Unless all productions are viewed critically there is the danger of praising a poor quality product. Recently an English teacher reported that he had recorded all of a currently broadcast series of Shakespeare's plays. Although several of the productions were less than second rate, he would be teaching those productions for years to come. Seeing a poor production of Shakespeare can do more harm than good, and may reinforce an audience member's contention that he is indeed a bore and his works as a whole of little interest. We must concede that we will use whatever means available in order to confront students with actual productions of the plays. Often live theatrical productions are not available to the teachers and rarely are they aligned with individual teaching schedules.

---

[285]Jay L. Halio, "This Wide and Universal Stage: Shakespeare's Plays as Plays," in *Teaching Shakespeare*, pp. 273-274.

Many teachers complain about this newer medium's disparity when compared to the live stage performance. McNamee is critical of this thinking.

> Ironically enough, when discussing a Shakespeare film, teachers will cite the difficulties of transmitting a play written for the Elizabethan stage to a different medium, a medium almost unnatural; yet we are trying to do something just as foreign and unnatural when we try to win Shakespeare via the printed page, a medium for which he rarely wrote and in which he had no particular interest.[286]

Most teachers agree that there is no substitute for live performances of the Bard's works. In Germany Shakespearean productions have been plentiful for several centuries. During an interview with Herman Goering in the 1930s, McNamee remarked that he had an excellent grasp of Shakespeare.

> When I asked, "Do you read Shakespeare a lot?" Goering answered, I rarely read him -- I listen to him. Later while studying in Germany I began to wonder if there was not a necessary connection between the German adulation of Shakespeare (Germany has more productions of the Bard in one year than England and the United States have together) and the fact that the German learns his Shakespeare from the boards of the theatre and not from the books of the classroom. I also began to wonder whether our limited classroom success (a success in noway commensurate with the time allotted or the wealth of Shakespeare) was not directly traceable to the overemphasis of the printed page, on the visual approach over against the auditory.[287]

As I suggested earlier, Shakespeare in performance can excite even a reticent student. It has been suggested that a visit to a production should culminate most classes in Shakespeare.

> In fact, since the fullest appreciation of a play comes with viewing a stage presentation of it, the teaching of Shakespeare *should be* initiated with the prospect of culmination in a visit to see this work. This is not easy. While repertory theatres are growing in number, many of their productions of the Bard are over the heads of our uninitiated youngsters, and a view of a difficult play would only lead to frustration and deaden further interest in the world's greatest playwright. However recent exception to this was the presentation of *The Winter's Tale* by the Shakespeare Company in Stratford, Connecticut. Difficult to read, this

---

[286]McNamee, "New Horizons in the Teaching of Shakespeare," p. 584.
[287]Ibid.

play was given such a clarifying and remarkable performance that the more than 250 youngsters whom I took to Stratford unanimously acclaimed it.[288]

Kenneth Kern, a member of the Board of Directors of the Indianapolis Shakespeare Festival, recently commented that Shakespeare "seems to cross age and socioeconomic lines." He had seen his first live production and noticed immediately how students sat in rapt attention during the two hour production. Many returned voluntarily to subsequent productions, seemingly enchanted by the magic of Shakespeare.[289]

> Inevitably, the teacher of Shakespeare is pitched into a quandary. On the one hand, he recognizes that seeing Shakespeare's plays staged or on film provides the utmost delight to audiences from all walks of life. (Often, at places like Ashland, Oregon's Shakespeare Festival, I have observed this phenomenon -- people from all over the West Coast and beyond, from small villages and big cities, from universities and shops, factories and farms, sitting enrapt at a dramatic performance of a tragedy or history, or breaking out in genuine laughter and delight at a fast paced comedy.) On the other hand, in the classroom the teacher finds his students grappling arduously with the texts of the very same plays, stumped by the language, the long dramatis personae (especially in the histories), or the sheer complexity of "interpretation." If honestly answering, few students -- or teachers, either -- would admit that they read Shakespeare for pleasure. It is work, hard work; and though it has its rewards, most would rather see a play than study it.[290]

Although Shakespeare remains the world's most staged playwright, productions do not occur as often as needed. Certainly, few teachers have the luxury of a stage play synchronized with their individual teaching schedules.

> But I soon realized that, although the opportunities for seeing Shakespeare produced seem to increase every year, they occur at random, as courses do not and thus can not be incorporated into them, at least not systematically.[291]

---

[288]Hanwerker, "When Should Shakespeare Be Taught in the Schools?" p. 71.

[289]Indianapolis City Council, Parks and Recreation Budget Committee Hearing, 19 August 1982.

[290]Halio, "This Wide and Universal Stage," p. 273.

[291]Eaves, "The Real Thing," p. 463.

Most critics agree that stage productions should not become classes in themselves, rather they should supplement academic teaching. Students must understand that the production they have witnessed is not the definitive stage version of the play. Any performance must be subjected to criticism from the teachers and the students. An individual production can always be illuminated by careful study and discussion of the script.

> These points being made, the analysis of particular productions should proceed. Ultimately, it probably does not matter very much whether students see the plays before or after they read them, although it is true that the initial effect of the production or the text will be different according to which proceeds the other. (I have not experimented adequately with 'the results of the different sequences to offer any meaningful data, but the matter might be worth exploring.) At any rate, eventually the student will have to compare the production he has seen with the modern edition he has read, possibly going on to compare several productions to each other as well as to the text. He is now in an excellent position to analyze both the play and his responses to it, responses which have become all the more vivid and personal because he has actively engaged in witnessing the play in action, in performance.[292]

I disagree with the above critic that the order of reading the script and viewing the performance matters little when considering the educational process. I have found that students who view the performance first are less willing to take the time for script study. They also return to class with many unalterable preconceptions. Often they will dislike the play if they did not enjoy the production. Serious analysis is very difficult in this situation. Though a thorough knowledge of the script can spoil the dramatic impact of the performance, a knowledgeable student is more suited to approach the production critically.

The question often arises when comparing performances and scripts: Why is the acting version so different from the edition used in class? Frequently stage performances are edited and adapted to suit the conceptions of the individual directors and the limitations of cast and theatre. "Practically every modern

---

[292]Halio, "This Wide and Universal Stage," pp. 278-279.

production is, in that sense, an adaptation."[293] If students are prepared for these changes, they are less apt to be disturbed during the performance. Although it is next to impossible to procure an individual acting version, a teacher can prepare a class with a general discussion about script adaptations. Many directors keep their young audience in mind when directing a production. I have even opened performances of Shakespearean plays to trial audiences of students in order to gauge the efficacy of comedy. "All this may sound like heresy to purists, but to students it awakens a keen sense of existential realities and plain common sense. 'Museum Shakespeare' is not for young minds."[294]

More than any other playwright Shakespeare is guarded by a multitude of academicians. Any changes are viewed with suspicion, inspite of the fact that a four hour "museum" *Romeo and Juliet* may permanently alienate a young mind. As said before, the discussion of the differences between script and performance have been found to be a valuable teaching aid to many teachers. Philip Traci writes: "That is, by analyzing the differences between text and production, we can arrive at more meaningful interpretations of the Shakespearean texts."[295] Traci was reviewing a production of *Hamlet* staged by Joseph Papp for New York Shakespeare Festival. His was an extremely modern approach with extensive revisions and substitutions. Very little of the original script remained.

> The most challenging of the questions raised by Papp's Happening, however, is that which is raised by Jan Kott, whom he quotes in his program notes: "One can perform only one of several Hamlets potentially existing in this arch play. It will always be a poorer *Hamlet* than Shakespeare's *Hamlet*, but it may also be a *Hamlet* enriched by being in our time. It may be, but I would rather say -- it must be so."[296]

Traci continues to defend the use of such productions as valuable tools for academic study. He quotes Joseph Papp as saying:

---

[293]Ibid., p. 277.

[294]Ibid., p. 276.

[295]Philip Traci, "Joseph Papp's Happening and the Teaching of *Hamlet*," *English Journal* 58 (January 1969): 77.

[296]Ibid.

My position is that they the students have the customary text of *Hamlet* as accepted by scholars and we are offering an interpretation of that text. Since the "straight" play is ambiguous, there is no conceivable way to produce it on stage without some special point of view.

I also hold the view that this production will challenge both teacher and student to tackle the written text in an imaginative and joyful way rather than through the old, tired, stale and dull methods generally taught in the city school systems.[297]

John Russell Brown agrees that Shakespeare must be recreated for the modern audience, in spite of the fact that in many ways he is an ardent Shakespeare purist.

He wrote plays for a kind of theatre that no longer exists and cannot be reconstructed. He wrote texts for actors to explore and recreate rather than for the solitary reader, and he was aware of an audience that shared its pleasures.[298]

The principle problem with formally staged productions remains their general inaccessibility to every teacher of Shakespeare. One way to introduce the Bard in performance is to utilize the actors at hand. The moment this possibility is suggested most educators of English literature react strongly. Class readings and productions seem to generate more controversy than any other educational approach to Shakespeare study. Often teachers not only doubt the students' ability but also their own in directing such projects. Walter Eggers feels that performances can be handled by the average teacher in the average class. "Performance is within the province of teachers of literature who recognize that the kinds of decisions they make as literary critics are involved in every theatrical production."[299] Eaves expresses the hesitation many teachers trained in English experience when approaching this technique.

The other alternative was some kind of class production. I was wary, since I knew that such a thing might take up more time than a whole shelf of phonograph records and waste a great deal more. But the

---

[297]Ibid., p. 75.

[298]Brown, *Free Shakespeare*, p. 2.

[299]Walter Eggers, "Introduction," in *Teaching Shakespeare*, p. xiii.

98

idea grew on me until I thought that beyond the hazards I could see an occasion for some very advanced teaching of Shakespeare.[300]

Some teachers started using class productions because they were frustrated by the arduous task of doing all the reading. Though these readings are not true class productions, they do expose students to the beauty of the spoken verse.

> Of course, for exploring longer speech, dialogues and more complicated interchanges between characters, more than one reader is almost essential and in a classroom or game situation, a small audience can replace the tape recorder with great advantage in immediately registering of effect and a quicker recognition of what is happening.[301]

Bernard Hanwerker recommends reading the whole play in class.

> The oral reading of the play itself should be done continuously (daily), with explanations regarding interpretation of language following each scene. General questions may be found in most text editions, but they can be edited and added to.

> In the oral reading, children should be assigned parts, rotating the assignment for the purpose of getting as many children as possible to participate. I have found that assigning girls to male parts in no way distracts the class from the study at hand, while allowing complete student participation. At the beginning the teacher may want to join in the reading (performing one of the major roles), thereby demonstrating to the children the dramatic quality and poetic interpretation or style of the writing.[302]

Brown is hesitant to endorse a complete production in the classroom. He believes that it is best to avoid "acting" as students read the text.

> The next development is to work on the same scene, introducing various uses of space and movement, and later of gesture and bearing. All this should be effected without calling on anyone's powers as an actor: indeed the tendency to perform should be gently inhibited at first, so that one or two participants do not run away with the game and so that everyone remains fully mobile in their readings and movement and able to respond objectively to what occurs. The object of the experiment is to awaken suggestions of how the scene might go, not to create a dramatic rendering. The decision to start acting may come later, when everyone is

---

[300]Eaves, "The Real Thing," p. 464.
[301]Brown, *Free Shakespeare*, p. 107.
[302]Hanwerker, "When Should Shakespeare be Taught in the Schools," p. 70.

ready and some few "interpretations" are ready for a final test of credibility. But at this point the experiment will be over.[303]

I find it hard to imagine that a teacher would want to suppress any kind of dramatic creativity on the part of the students. It is Brown's intention to focus all the attention on the verse, but a flat reading of a dramatic piece can work against the expression of meaning. Without plot to support the poetry the whole experience can be lost. Halio disagrees that this type of reading should be the end of the process:

> After several years of experimentation, I have found that the requirement of a scene or parts of scenes lasting at least fifteen or twenty minutes and staged entirely by students in small groups of five, six, or seven members each, works well. In my experience it has proved more valuable than the traditional term paper,...[304]

He continues to explain the structure of such a project and stresses one important point.

> Each group of students must choose a scene that it wishes to present, either from a play studied in class or from one selected and read on their own (advantages and disadvantages either way usually balance out). Lines must be memorized.[305]

It is interesting to note the stress placed on memorization and recitation by the Elizabethan schoolmasters. In spite of John Russell Brown's scholarship in the life and times of Shakespeare he ardently resists committing verse to memory. He is not the only critic to deny the value of memorization. Reestablishment of an oral tradition in education has often been proposed, but this suggestion is also denounced by teachers and critics alike as busywork.

> Ask students to memorize! It is very popular to condemn memorization as the bane of the English Students, the curse of the program. Yet, those persons who most vocally deplore the assignment are also the most proficient at delivering the very lines which they purportedly resent having to commit to the treasure-house of memory and the enrichment of their oratory. Surely it is through Shakespeare, above all,

---

[303]Brown, *Free Shakespeare*, p. 107.
[304]Halio, "This Wide and Universal Stage," p. 784.
[305]Ibid., p. 785.

we acquire the sound of great poetic language and acquire the standard by which to measure our own limited rhetorical range.[306]

The fear may arise in the teachers that they are not really teaching, merely spending their time being an audience to the class experimentation. Halio tries to allay these fears.

> By the end of the term, if the instructor is fortunate, he will discover that he has become superfluous. Which is another way of saying that both he and his students have done their work and done it well.[307]

The reason many teachers resist performance in class is a fear that focus will shift away from the text. This may be true, but Heilman believes that both the class and the teacher have a lot to gain.

> There are limits to what a teacher whose degree is in literature can do with machinery even of the most sophisticated kind, and certain other essays are emphatic in arguing against wasting class time this way...We have given the last word to the theatrical side not to resolve the dispute but to stress its importance. The teacher of literature should be warned that to conceive of drama as performance may mean to shift its fundamental assumptions about the stability and integrity of the literary text; he and his students will have to pay closer attention than they usually do to the effects on an audience of the moment-by-moment progress of the play.[308]

Several critics have recommended that teachers should balance the performance with some academic presentations on the part of the teacher.

> While he is learning, the student should learn not only about literary scholarship, and his learning should have both a practical foreground and a theoretical background.[309]

Eaves breaks the class into groups which are responsible for every aspect of theatrical production. He then mounts a complete production in the classroom: "To meet these criteria, the project took the form of a learning 'program' with four interlocking parts: texts, sets and costumes, acting and directing, and

---

[306]Veidemanis, "Shakespeare in the High School Classroom," p. 59.
[307]Halio, "This Wide and Universal Stage," p. 286.
[308]Eggers, "Introduction," pp. xii-xiii.
[309]Eaves, "The Real Thing," p. 464.

reviewing."[310] He reports that this acquaints the students with many aspects of theatrical production. After the production the students sit down and listen to detailed reviews presented by the review section and in turn give their reactions to the reviewers' statements. This method seems to incorporate the entire class while allowing those with no propensity for performance the freedom to engage in other activities.

More conservative teachers are worried that performance of any kind will distract the students from serious study of the script.

> Thus it is that the idea of performance, not performance as such, has place in the classroom. Although our stress is heavy, as John Russell Brown and others have taught us that it should be, we would not overdo it. Our minds tend to fix on the modern or eccentric. And there is a limit to how adequately we can represent in the classroom successful performance, even when we imagine or have experienced such.[311]

The last sentence written by the above critic suggests an inherent fear of production in the classroom. It seems to state that when education becomes exciting and involves the imaginations of the students it must be suspect. Again we are faced with the old conflict between Shakespeare as literature and Shakespeare as theatre.

Another method of classroom presentation is detailed by Martha Treichler. After receiving unanimous disapproval from her class when she mentioned reading Shakespeare aloud, she proposed a compromise, "Read it yourselves, outside of class, then, but be prepared to come to class and act out in your own words what happens between characters."[312] When they returned to class after their home study, their teacher asked them to perform. They were unable to do so without their books, so the teacher allowed them to work from open scripts. They improvised the action in their own words which included liberal use of slang and colloquialisms. She encouraged other students to interrupt the proceedings

---

[310]Ibid.

[311]Carroll, "The Presentation of Shakespeare," p. 60.

[312]Treichler, "Free Acting Shakespeare," p. 64.

.with criticisms and reminders of left-out material. The final day of the study was dedicated to acting out the whole play in a general manner without the use of books. The idea of this hour long contemporary condensation might disturb some critics. Certainly, the product was far removed from the Shakespearean text, but Martha Treichler reports considerable success.

> But although progress was not so fast nor so dramatic as I had envisioned it, it was an exciting change from a question-and-answer class. Once in a while, someone would render a whole paragraph in his own words without looking at the book. And once in a while, a couple of students would get interested and put honest, believable expression into their parts. Their comments on the characters were shrewd, and usually highly critical.[313]

I utilized a similar project with the apprentices of the California Shakespeare Festival (1978) in rehearsal for their production of *The Two Gentlemen of Verona*. These were advanced students, all with strong aspirations towards professional theatre. During three, one hour periods, these twenty actors improvised the entire play scene by scene. The exercise proved very enlightening for the students. The plot was immediately clarified and line meanings were discovered by group interaction. One must remember that these were theatre-oriented students, but as one method of script study, improvisation can be successful.

While this experiment was used in a performance training program, the utilization of theatre techniques in literature classes has been criticized by many English teachers. Their criticisms generally fall into three categories. First, they worry that students are not skilled enough to manage the Elizabethan verse.

> It is true, the teacher can utilize class members to perform scenes, and there is considerable value to be gained by the student actor's effort to perform the text. In the main, however, it takes highly skilled actors to illustrate Shakespeare's drama effectively.[314]

---

[313]Ibid.

[314]Beckerman, "Shakespeare's Plays as Works of Drama," p. 314.

Admittedly, scene studies staged by students in the classroom are not going to compare with the performances of trained professionals. Education is often too product oriented, and English teachers are trained to expect the perfect essay from their students. J. L. Styan envisions the product of class performances: "...twenty freshmen...become ten Lears and ten Cordelias."[315] There is a temptation by the teacher to make the production look professional by overproducing the experiment. Even those who favor performance work may discourage other educators from approaching the task lightly. "Acting, especially in Shakespeare's plays, is not as easy as it can sometimes look: educational productions are complicated exercises that make huge physical and psychological demands."[316]

The second most popular technique concerns the education of the English teachers. Most of them are not trained to coach acting and very few have studied the fundamentals of stagecraft and production. It is ironic that so many of these unskilled professionals are heading the theatre programs in American high schools. Their training in oral skills may also be lacking. "...teachers are seldom skilled enough to illustrate their remarks through comparative readings of their own."[317]

Some teachers insist that these types of educational techniques are outside of their discipline. "The English teacher should not be forced to be the drama teacher also,..."[318] Brown also agrees that it is an unusual teacher who will not be tempted to expect a professional product from his students:

> Only a very wise teacher-director can keep a balance between aspiration and achievement, and only a few of those involved will learn as much about Shakespeare as they do about themselves as actors and

---

[315]J.L. Styan, "Direct Method Shakespeare," *Shakespeare Quarterly* 25 (1974): 199.
[316]Brown, *Free Shakespeare*, p. 49.
[317]Beckerman, "Shakespeare's Play as Works of Drama," p. 314.
[318]Diesman, "Shakespeare in High School Today," p. 132.

about the difficulties of theatre production without adequate training, facilities or time.[319]

Brown goes on to comment that many teachers who are not experienced in production tend to compliment everything and this can be very misleading for the student and his perception of Shakespeare.

> Alternatively, the student actors can be protected from criticism and come away from the experience thinking that they have effected wonders and be more pleased with themselves than excited by Shakespeare.[320]

The third, and usually the most intense criticism, concerns the perceived purpose of traditional literary study. Teachers are often adamant about utilizing only established educational techniques when studying Shakespeare.

> I try to get classes themselves to understand from the beginning: what we are doing here is studying, not reading as we want to; carefully taking apart and partly putting together, not immediately mastering a whole. A class is not a theatre; it can not be and should not be. Studying a play can not be like seeing it on the stage (or hearing it on a disk or tape). It can not be immediately satisfying, gratifying, fulfilling as can be the whole or finished play. In class we stop, focus, repeat, go back, examine and reexamine, look about, look under, search, test, give up, start over: everything that we can not do in theatre. What we do in class is "unnatural" and "abnormal" -- if , that is, the process is compared with seeing a play, or even with an ordinary reading of it.[321]

I question the rationale of telling his students that the next assignment is going to be less than exciting. It would be extremely hard to inspire a class prepared by such a declaration. Teachers often seem threatened by new teaching methods. Some infer that an instructor is not really doing his job if the students do the majority of the reading.

> ...yet an English class for young people must be more than a mock theatre where children learn by doing. Shakespeare is Shakespeare with all the implications that the statement entails. I am not opposed to acting

---

[319]Brown, *Free Shakespeare*, p. 105.
[320]Ibid.
[321]Heilman, "Shakespeare in the Classroom," p. 14.

nor any other device, including the carving of Shakespearean characters in soap, but the teacher should be able to do more than assign parts.[322]

The above comment is typical of many English teachers. They seem to have a very denigrating attitude towards performance in the classroom. No advocate of classroom productions feels that they should be staged without supplemental academic study. John Russell Brown's comments about the lack of critical examination when a class reviews their own production may have some validity. Martha Treichler is exuberant in her praise of class productions; however she does recognize the class's tendency to give themselves rave reviews.

> They seemed to be enjoying themselves thoroughly. There was, especially on the second day, a gradual relaxing and freeing of the atmosphere. It was noisy. There were shouts "You forgot this!" There was laughter when someone translated Shakespeare into vivid colloquial American. When we finished I asked them how they felt they had done.

> "We all did wonderful," they said. (sic)

> They complimented each other. One said to me. "You did well, Martha!" (I had filled in occasionally as a messenger.)[323]

This same teacher admitted that there were peripheral rewards to this oral exercise. These exercises established a new verbal tradition in her classroom. Although some critics feel that the improvement of communication practices may not be applicable to the study of Shakespeare, I am amazed at the number of English teachers who confess frustration when it comes to stimulating discussion in their literature classes. Treichler reported a marked improvement:

> As so often happens with student-centered teaching, we learned more than the students thought. What I saw happening was a general loosening of tongues and a freeing of words. To my amazement I continued afterward to see a marked improvement in their ease and skill at expressing themselves orally. This was perhaps the most important learning that came from acting out the play. Our class discussions underwent a permanent improvement which lasted the rest of the year.

---

[322]Marder, "Teaching Shakespeare," p. 485.
[323]Treichler, "Free Acting Shakespeare," p. 65.

They had learned something about Shakespeare's play, too, and at the end of our study they could express his ideas in their own words, which was an indication to me that they had made a beginning in learning to understand Shakespeare's language.[324]

Many teachers might argue that these students, while increasing their verbal proficiency, did not acquaint themselves with either Shakespeare or his works to any great extent. This exercise did teach them something about the characters and a synopsis of the plots. Treichler's students appeared to be engrossed in the project. Those with a propensity for performance obviously dominated the action, but she reports that others benefitted.

(While performing *The Merchant of Venice* she) asked the other students to play the courtroom scene. The latter performed so well, deftly changing scarves as he changed characters, that we gave him a round of applause as he finished. The other two non-performers also showed an adequate grasp of the play.[325]

Although many teachers report positive results from production experimentation, Mary Hyde Rowan polled her students after a similar project and received mixed responses:

Three students disliked it, admitting that they worked best under the threat of grades, liked having someone else plan for them, and were unwilling to accept responsibility for setting their own goals and budgeting their time. The rest loved it! I felt that they learned valuable lessons about studying, research, and independent planning, and that they enjoyed the play much more than they would have without the background work which they had imposed on themselves.[326]

This teacher felt that such an exercise could only be valid if the freedom of this student responsibility extended into the grading process:

After a few deprecatory remarks and my assurance that modesty should be subordinate to pride of accomplishment, each student told me

---

[324] Ibid.

[325] Ibid., p. 65.

[326] Mary Hyde Rowan, "A do it yourself kit: Ninth Graders 'Run' the English Class," *Clearing House* 38 (1964): 375.

what he thought his grade should be. There was not one I would have changed![327]

Martha Treichler reported that some of her students were apprehensive about continuing this method in the future. She received mixed reactions on her production experimentation.

> I asked them, on our last day, what they thought of this way of studying Shakespeare. Most of them stated positively that they preferred it; some were not sure; and one lady stated, "If I liked the play, I would really want to study it like this. But if I didn't like it, then I rather just read it, take a test on it, and get it over with." This indicated to me that it was harder for them to stay uninvolved, it was harder to "just get it over with" quickly, when they themselves just acted out Shakespeare.[328]

This indicates that many of her students approached reading Shakespeare as a task which had to be completed as painlessly as possible. Most students expect literature to bore them; this initial attitude of doubt is the first obstacle for the teacher of Shakespeare.

Possibly the most rewarding experience was reported by Morris Eaves. Suddenly his "homework" became a personal experience. Students often motivated other students to complete their obligations to the project. The class became an ensemble with the production project as the unifying force.

> ...students who collaborate to solve their problems, and thus witness the interest and dedication of others at a closer range and for a longer time than usual, quickly interested and dedicated themselves. Thus "homework" -- a word and an attitude that many students bring with them from high school -- becomes "my work" much earlier than usual in a student's university career. And they learn meanwhile...that the "real thing" is the "acted and felt play" -- Shakespeare intact.[329]

For most students who experience Shakespeare's poetry, as opposed to adlibbing his plots, they internalize the rhythm and magic of his verse during recitation. We are reminded time and again that he wrote words to be recited:

---

[327]Ibid.
[328]Treichler, "Free Acting Shakespeare," p. 65.
[329]Eaves, "The Real Thing," p. 471.

"Shakespeare wrote his plays to be heard rather than read. His language has the freedom, irregularity and self-indulgence of spoken English."[330]

Many have implied that this oral method could be applied to other forms of literature. "I believe the answer to many of our literary problems in education is to be found in making the student listen to his own voice."[331] Recitation will not be a cure-all for the lazy student, but it offers teachers another way to reach their class. Reading becomes an aural event more closely allied to singing. "...once the human ear is titillated by the melodious magic that is Shakespeare, then Shakespeare (and what Shakespeare is saying) becomes part of him for life and he is never the same again."[332] This new love of sound and rhythm in the Bard's plays can be transferred to the study of other types of literature. I would assert that the primary need for the actor and for the literary student alike is to listen to his own vocal dramatization -- which the *Four Quartets* need every bit as much as Shakespeare if a public reading it is attempted -- and see how it works.[333] Even the detractors cannot argue that this experience is primary, where the silent reading at home is definitely secondary. "Hence the significance of a technique that fosters the play of active intelligence and sensibility, as against other techniques which promote a more passive acceptance of second-hand insights, however authoritative."[334] Indeed, many of the explanations and clarification of theme and content which occupy the majority of class time may become irrelevant with the introduction of additional oral reading techniques. Action makes many of the incongruities immediately reconcilable. "Dramatic conventions offer a convenient shorthand that frees the playwright from laborious explanations."[335] This may awaken in the student something more -- an experience that can enable him to appreciate other arts.

---

[330]Charney, "How to Read Shakespeare," p. 54.

[331]G. Wilson Knight, "The Teacher as Poetic Actor," in *Teaching Shakespeare*, p. 293.

[332]McNamee, "New Horizons in Teaching Shakespeare," p. 585.

[333]Knight, "the Teacher as Poetic Actor," p. 304.

[334]Halio, "This Wide and Universal Stage," p. 288.

[335]Charney, "How to Read Shakespeare," p. 33.

But this auditory approach gives one more thing over and above the elucidation of text and clarification of character; it gives the effect -- the aesthetic experience! Could we ask for more?[336]

The students experience the art of the theatre whether they read aloud, act out the parts, or witness a live presentation. They learn that theatre is different from television and other dramatic media. They also begin to appreciate what is essentially dramatic in the plays of Shakespeare.

> They also learned something about drama. When they acted out what was happening in the play they began to see that drama was composed of the reactions and the responses of one or more persons to the feelings and actions of others. They saw that it was more than just memorized lines. This became especially clear when they wanted to take the play in a direction other than Shakespeare's...They could see that each character had a special personality which determined the way he would react to situations and other personalities.[337]

Or as T.S. Elliot wrote in *Seneca in Elizabethan Translation*, "... the acted and felt play...is always the real thing. The phrase, beautiful as it may be, stands for a greater beauty still."[338]

This approach to the plays of Shakespeare should not exclude textual study. Charney concludes that the two methods should be used together. "We need to pursue both text and subtext simultaneously, so that our perspective is not limited by the verbal form in which the play is set down."[339] This is an aspect that many proponents of the oral form fail to acknowledge; textual study does contribute immeasurably to a student's appreciation of the play.

In order to balance the study between the seeming extremes of literature and presentation, we may need to develop a new type of teacher: a drama teacher with a strong academic and historical background. I have often noted that English teachers express an animosity towards staged Shakespeare.

---

[336]McNamee, "New Horizons in Teaching Shakespeare," p. 585.
[337]Treichler, "Free Acting Shakespeare," p. 65.
[338]Eaves, "The Real Thing," p. 463.
[339]Charney, "How to Read Shakespeare," p. 15.

> Finding an instructor competent to teach both acting and Shakespeare without turning the first into an exercise in discovering and interpreting image clusters or the second into an excuse for playing his John Gielgud records would admittedly be a difficult task. Yet establishing the opportunity for a scholar to live with the body and the soul of drama would certainly help to create a full dramatic-academic man.[340]

Maintaining this balance is as hard for teachers of theatre as it is for those of English. Drama teachers often succumb to the temptation to make the classroom a stage. The production is complete with lights, sound, music, and severed paper-mache heads. The focus of the class becomes the completion of a product for an audience (even if only the teacher and class witness the event), and the process of education may suffer. "The emphasis on elaborate and frequent productions has often kept the theatre faculty and students too busy for thorough research."[341] Once anyone attempts to mount a production of any magnitude the process immediately becomes complicated.

> Everyone must concede that drama is messy. As opposed to the tidy activity of reading a poem, the proper recreation of drama involved hammering and sawing, the slapping on of paint, and the waste of evening after evening rehearsing the absurd pretense that you are someone else.[342]

In spite of the "messy" nature of theatrical education, Barry concedes that the time may be ripe for shifting all the Shakespeare courses from English to the Theatre Department. Although his suggestion is meant to be ironic, it contains some serious accusations against the present methods of teaching the plays of William Shakespeare.

> ...there is as much logic in allowing a drama department to teach the campus Shakespeare courses as in letting English have them ...Academic committees...would see little positive point and a great deal

---

[340]Jackson G. Barry, "The Day the English Department Gave Up Shakespeare," *Journal of Higher Education* 38 (January 1967): 83.

[341]Ibid., p. 81.

[342]Ibid., p. 78.

of possible harm in having courses in Shakespeare taught in the drama department.[343]

> ...If the drama department is not to get Shakespeare, perhaps the English Department could take him back -- but as a man restored to what he actually was, a working dramatist who used the stage, not the book, as his medium.

> This is indeed to drift above the hard realities of academic life; for, if pressed to respond to as naive a suggestion as the one I have just made, many English professors would confess that they have tolerated Shakespeare all these years precisely because they have been allowed to regard him as a poet, not as a dramatist.[344]

Those English teachers who admit the effectiveness of presentation techniques also underline the necessity for research criticism and analysis. The ideal method, if there is one, seems to be a blending of the two departments and the team teaching of Shakespeare courses.

> But there are at present limitations to such a method (performance in the class). Many of us feel, as a matter partly of instinct and partly of experience that for most undergraduates Shakespeare's poetry, however well performed, nonetheless requires analysis; That specific scenes need to be fitted into large, sometimes abstract, structures which students can not see without help; that getting at Shakespeare demands to some extent an Elizabethan perspective we ought to teach; and that his wide range effect on Western culture it is our duty at least to suggest.[345]

While the drama teachers might be eager to enter into the English class and share their methods with the students, it seems that the English teachers might be hesitant to permit this. While these types of amalgamated teaching methods may never be fully exploited in high schools and colleges, the summer Shakespeare programs connected with festivals may allow other experimentation.

The older controversy among English teachers has always centered upon the method of dealing with the script. My experience testifies that many English

---

[343]Ibid.

[344]Ibid., p. 82.

[345]Carroll, "The Presentation of Shakespeare," p. 50.

teachers work either by examining the historical context or by analysis and criticism of the play. Heilman disposes of these exclusive systems.

> But by now the history-vs.-criticism match-up has been worked to death and can not shed much light on what goes on in Shakespeare teaching; in fact, as I will propose later, these two rivals have more to bring them together on a side than to make them challenge each other. We can get better sense of practices and options. I think, by involving -- only, that is, as an instrument of exploration -- another opposed pair that perhaps better describe the current problem: Shakespeare as scientific object and Shakespeare as immediate experience.[346]

This may be the difference between teaching the Bard as an experience in performance or as literature. Surely a production is immediate and reading tends to be analytical. The study of the plays in class, however, does not have to be over-loaded with confusing criticism. Can these works be studied as dramatic performances, and can modern educators make these plays jump off the printed page into the hearts of their student? It has often been theorized that Shakespeare may have spent some time as a teacher in the Stratford school. If this were the case, he must have confronted the problem of exciting his students about their daily readings and memorizations. He may have felt the same frustrations when discussing classical works as modern educators experience with his plays. We would hope that he would feel some empathy for teachers and their predicaments.

> Aubrey's legend that Shakespeare was a teacher, a "schoolmaster in the country," before he became an actor and playwright is irresistible to Shakespeare teachers, who like to think that they would have his sympathy. Yet the only memorable teacher in Shakespeare's plays is Holofernes in *Love's Labour's Lost*, a vain and dogmatic pedant.[347]

After examining the educational approaches to the Bard in secondary schools, we are left with varying methods, but it is obvious that Shakespearean study is primarily textual. Most teachers use a method which gets the students to read the play the night before an announced quiz. This testing is followed by a

---

[346]Heilman, "Shakespeare in the Classroom," pp. 5-6.
[347]Eggers, "Introduction," p. xi.

discussion of plot and poetic symbols. An active participatory approach is seldom used by secondary educators.

In short, the teachers must learn how to let their students take the initiative with Shakespeare. Years of failure have shown that traditional methods have not achieved an appreciation of Shakespeare and his plays. We, as educators, must generate a more participatory program of study. Students should realize that Shakespeare's plays are not exclusively great literary works, rather they are blueprints for theatrical production. When witnessed on stage his plays have a vitality which can only be imagined when studied in a textbooks. Only through a participatory approach can Shakespeare's plays make an impression on young minds. Encouraging questions, comments and criticism is integral to the learning experience. It is vitally important that we educate teachers in the methods of dealing with Shakespeare in the classroom. Teachers and students should be encouraged to attend live Shakespearean productions. Study guides and visits by professional actors and directors can prepare students for the experience of live theatre. We must break down the barriers of "Bardolotry" that keep teachers from sharing his humanity with their classes. When young students experience this vibrant, alive, playwright at an early age, love for his writing will stay with them all their lives.

BIBLIOGRAPHY

Ashton, Geoffrey, *The Collector's Shakespeare: His Life and Work in Paintings, Prints and Photographs*, New York: Random House, 1990.

Baldwin, T.W., *The Organization and Personnel of the Shakespearean Company*, New York: Russell and Russell, 1961.

Barry, Jackson G., "The Day the English Department Gave Up Shakespeare," *Journal of Higher Education* 38, January 1967.

Bartholomeusz, Dennis, *Macbeth and the Players*, London: Cambridge University Press, 1969.

Beckerman, Bernard, *Shakespeare at the Globe: 1599-1609*, New York: The MacMillan Company, 1962.

Beckerman, Bernard, "Shakespeare's Plays as Works of Drama," in *Teaching Shakespeare*, Edens, Walter et. al. eds., Princeton, NJ: Princeton University Press, 1977.

Blackwell, William, Manuscript from the Folger Library Special Collection, 1595.

Bradbrook, M.C., *The Rise of the Common Player: A Study of Actor and Society in Shakespeare's England*, Cambridge: Mass.: Harvard University Press, 1961.

Brown, Ivor, *How Shakespeare Spent the Day*, New York: Hill and Wang, 1963.

Brown, Ivor, *Shakespeare and the Actors*, London: The Bodley Head, 1970.

Brown, Ivor, *The Women in Shakespeare's Life*, New York: Coward McCann, Inc., 1969.

Brown, John Russell, *Free Shakespeare*, London: Heineman Press, 1974.

Carroll, D. Allen, "The Presentation of Shakespeare," in Wright, *Shakespeare in School and College*, Champaign, IL: National Council of Teachers of English, 1964.

Charney, Maurice, *How to Read Shakespeare*, New York: McGraw-Hill, 1971.

Chute, Marchette, *Shakespeare of London*, New York: E.P. Dutton and Company, 1949.

Cook, Judith, *Women in Shakespeare*, London: Harrup Limited, 1980.

Davies, W. Robertson, *Shakespeare's Boy Actors*, New York: Russell and Russell, Inc., 1964.

Dent, Alan, *World of Shakespeare: Sports and Pastimes*, New York: Taplinger Publishing Company, 1974.

Diesman, Florence M., "Shakespeare in High School Today," *Journal of Secondary Education* 40, March 1965.

Dusinberre, Juliet, *Shakespeare and the Nature of Women*, London: The MacMillan Press, 1975.

Eaves, Morris, "The Real Thing: A Plan for Producing Shakespeare in the Classroom," *College English* 31, February 1970.

Edens, Walter; Durer, Christopher; Eggers, Walter; Harris, Duncan; and Hull,Keith, eds., *Teaching Shakespeare*, Princeton, NJ: Princeton University Press, 1977.

Edgecombe, David, *Educational Programs of Four North American Shakespeare Festivals*, Doctoral Dissertation: Kent State University, 1986.

Edgecombe, David, Survey by the author taken at *The Indianapolis Shakespeare Festival*, July 29, 1992.

Eggers, Walter, "Introduction," in *Teaching Shakespeare*, Edens, Walter et. al. eds., Princeton, NJ: Princeton University Press, 1977.

Farrant, Richard, An Autographed letter signed to William Moore, London, August 27, 1574. Folger Library Special Collection.

Fraser, Russell A., *Shakespeare: The Later Years*, New York: Columbia University Press, 1972.

Gurr, Andrew, *The Shakespearean Stage: 1574 to 1642*, London: The Cambridge University Press, 1970.

Halio, Jay L., "This Wide and Universal Stage: Shakespeare's Plays as Plays," in *Teaching Shakespeare*, Edens, Walter et. al. eds., Princeton, NJ: Princeton University Press, 1977.

Halliday, F.E., *Shakespeare and His Age*, New York: Thomas Yoeseloff, 1956.

Halliwell-Phillips Scrapbooks, vol. "Childrens Companies," Folger Library Special Collection.

Halliwell-Phillips Scrapbooks, vol. "Minor Actors," Folger Library Special Collection.

Hamilton, A.C., "The Case of Measure for Measure," in *Teaching Shakespeare*, Edens, Walter, et. al. eds., Princeton, NJ: Princeton University Press, 1977.

Harrison, G.B., *Elizabethan Plays and Players*, Ann Arbor, Michigan: The University of Michigan Press, 1956.

Harbage, Alfred, *Shakespeare's Audience*, New York: Columbia University Press, 1961.

Heeden, Barbara, "Shakespeare in First Grade," *Grade Teacher* 82, October 1964.

Heilman, Robert B., "Shakespeare in the Classroom," in *Teaching Shakespeare*, Edens, Walter et. al., eds., Princeton, NJ: Princeton University Press, 1977.

Hanwerker, Bernard, "When Should Shakespeare be Taught in the Schools," *High Points*, March 1961.

Hillebrand, Harold Newcombe, *The Children Actors*, New York: Russell and Russell, 1964.

Hodges, C. Walter, *Shakespeare and the Players*, London: G. Bell and Sons, 1970.

Indianapolis City Council, Parks and Recreation Budget Committee Hearing, 19 August 1982.

Introduction to *The Holy Bible* Revised Standard Version, New York: Thomas Nelson and Sons, 1952.

Kemp, William, *The Education of Children in Learning*, London: Thomas Orwin, 1588. Folger Library Special Collection.

Jones, John, *The Arts and Science of Perfering Bodie and Soule in al Health, Wisdom, and Catholic Religion*, London: Ralph Newberrie, 1579. Folger Library Special Collection.

Knight, G. Wilson, "The Teacher as Poetic Actor," in *Teaching Shakespeare*, Edens, Walter et. al. eds., Princeton, NJ: Princeton University Press, 1977.

Knights, L.C., *Drama and Society in the Age of Jonson*, London: Chatto and Windus, Ltd., 1937.

Leech, Clifford, *The Revels History of Drama in English*, 3 vols., London: Methuen and Company, 1957.

Marder, Louis, "Teaching Shakespeare: Is There a Method?" *College English* 25, April 1964.

McNamee, Laurence, "New Horizons in the Teaching of Shakespeare," *College English* 23, April 1962.

Moore, Peter, *The Apprentice Warningpiece*, London: 1641.

Nungezer, Edwin, *A Dictionary of Actors Before 1641*, New York: Greenwood Press, 1929.

Pitt, Angela, *Shakespeare's Women*, London: Newton Abbot, 1981.

Plimpton, George A., *The Education of Shakespeare*, London: Oxford University Press, 1933.

Pohl, Frederick J., *Like to the Lark: The Early Years of Shakespeare*, New York: Clarkson N. Potter, Inc., 1972.

Raleigh, Sir Walter; Lee, Sir Sidney; and Onions, Charles Talbut, eds., *Shakespeare's England: An Account of Life and Manners*, London: Claredon Press, 1962.

Reese, M.M., *Shakespeare and His World and Work*, New York: St. Martin's Press, Inc., 1953.

Rowan, Mary Hyde, "A Do it Yourself Kit: Ninth Graders 'Run' the English Class," *Clearing House* 38, 1964.

Rowse, A,L., *Eminent Elizabethans*, Athens, GA: The University of Georgia Press, 1983.

Rowse, A.L., Introduction to *The Annotated Shakespeare*, New York: Clark N. Potter, Inc., 1978.

Schelling, Felix, *Elizabethan Drama: 1558-1642*, New York: Russell and Russell, 1935; reprint ed. 1959.

Schoenbaum, S., *Shakespeare's Lives*, New York: Oxford University Press, 1991.

Schoenbaum, S., *William Shakespeare: A Compact Documentary Life*, New York: Oxford University Press, 1977.

___, *Shakespeare: The Globe and the World*, New York: Oxford University Press, 1991.

___, *Shakespeare's Players*, London: Harrup Limited, 1983.

Shapiro, Michael, *Children of Revels: The Boy Companies of Shakespeare's Time and Their Plays*, New York: Columbia University Press, 1977.

Spain, Delbert, *Shakespeare Sounded Soundly*, Santa Barbara, CA: Capra Press, 1988.

Speaight, Robert, *Shakespeare: The Man and His Achievement*, New York: Stein and Day Publishers, 1977.

Styan, J.L., "Direct Method Shakespeare," *Shakespeare Quarterly* 25, 1974.

Traci, Philip, "Joseph Papp's Happening and the Teaching of *Hamlet*," *English Journal* 58, January 1969.

Treichler, Martha, "Free Acting Shakespeare," *The Independent School Bulletin* 31, May 1972.

Veidemanis, Glayds, "Shakespeare in the High School Classroom," in Wright, *Shakespeare in School and College*, Champaign, IL: National Council of Teachers of English, 1964.

Vickers, Brian, "Teaching Coriolanus: The Importance of Perspective," in *Teaching Shakespeare*, Edens, Walter, et. al. eds., Princeton, NJ: Princeton University Press, 1977.

Webster, Margaret, *Shakespeare Today*, London: Dent Publishers, 1957.

Werthern, Albert, "The Reteaching and Regreening of Macbeth," in *Teaching Shakespeare*, Edens, Walter et. al. eds., Princeton, NJ: Princeton University Press. 1977.

Wilson, Edwin, *Shaw on Shakespeare*, New York: Dodd, Mead and Company, 1961.

Whitaker, Virgil K., *Shakespeare's Use of Learning*, San Marino, California: the Huntington Library Press, 1953.

Wright, Louis B., "Shakespeare for Everyman," in *Shakespeare in School and College*, ed. National Council of Teachers of English, Champaign, IL: National Council of Teachers of English, 1964.

____, *Young Shakespeare*, New York: Columbia University Press, 1988.

INDEX